VISIT ST

The Ultimate Guide to Stockholm Sightseeing Wonders, Itineraries, Tips, Travel Inspiration and Rich History of Stockholm.

Becky Rhodes

Copyright © 2023 by Becky Rhodes

All rights reserved

No part of this publication may be reproduced, stored in a retrieval system, or transmitted in any form or by any means, electronic, mechanical, photocopying, recording, or otherwise, without the prior written permission of the publisher, except in the case of brief quotations embodied in critical reviews and certain other noncommercial uses permitted by copyright law.

TABLE OF CONTENT

WELCOME TO STOCKHOLM _____ 6
   The Top 7 Reasons to Visit Stockholm! _____ 7

CHAPTER ONE _____ 13
   Travel Advice for Visiting Stockholm _____ 13
   Stockholm Etiquette - What to Do and What Not to Do in Stockholm _____ 18
   What to Do and What Not to Do _____ 21
   15 Things to Do and See in Stockholm _____ 24
   Must-See Parks & Gardens in Stockholm _____ 32
   Make the Most of Your Stockholm Summer _____ 37

CHAPTER TWO _____ 49
   Advice and Information on Travel Planning _____ 50
   Visa and Passport Requirements _____ 52
   Travel Essentials and Tips for Stockholm _____ 58
   When Is the Best Time to Visit Stockholm? _____ 62
   Useful Phrases and Words for Travelers _____ 71

CHAPTER THREE _____ 79
   Best Places to Eat in Stockholm for Locals _____ 81
   Best Stockholm Foods for Everyone _____ 89
   The Top 9 Fika Cafés in Stockholm _____ 98

CHAPTER FOUR _____ 105
   Stockholm Transportation Guide _____ 109
   Road Trips Around Stockholm _____ 112

CHAPTER FIVE _____ 119

- Stockholm's Best Islands _____ 121
- Stockholm's Best Hotels _____ 128
- Stockholm's Best Airbnbs _____ 136
- Stockholm Budget Hotels _____ 141

CHAPTER SIX _____ *149*
- The Best Boat Tours & Cruises in Stockholm _____ 151
- 18 Of Stockholm's Top Boat Trips and Cruises _____ 155
- What to Bring on a Boat Tour _____ 161

CHAPTER SEVEN _____ *165*
- The Top 8 Hikes in Stockholm _____ 165
- Simple Hikes in Stockholm _____ 170

CHAPTER EIGHT _____ *173*
- Making the Most of Family Adventures When Traveling with Children _____ 173
- Stockholm's Best Family-Friendly Locations _____ 176
- Activities for Children in Stockholm _____ 183

CHAPTER NINE _____ *193*
- Stockholm's Best Lakes and Beaches _____ 196
- The 5 Best Subway Art in Stockholm _____ 204
- Stockholm's Most Instagrammable Locations _____ 208

CHAPTER TEN _____ *218*
- Stockholm's Most Popular Neighborhoods _____ 219
- 5 Essential Advice for Newcomers Visiting Stockholm Nightlife _____ 227
- Stockholm's Nightclubs _____ 230
- 10 Cheap Ways to Visit Stockholm _____ 242

Book Your Trip to Stockholm: Logistical Hints and Tips _____ 248

Best Shopping Locations in Stockholm _____ 249

Shopping in Stockholm: 18 Amazing Swedish Souvenirs! _____ 256

WELCOME TO STOCKHOLM

Stockholm stands as one of the world's most exquisite capitals. The city is breathtakingly positioned by the Baltic Sea and is the picturesque capital of Sweden, where history and modernity dance together along the shores of its archipelago, built on 14 islands surrounding one of Europe's largest and best-preserved medieval city cores. Stockholm, founded in the mid-13th century, has long been recognized as a cultural light in Scandinavia, lauded for its devotion to innovation, sustainability, and design.

Gamla Stan (the Old Town)'s cobblestone alleyways and ochre-colored buildings whisper tales of medieval times, while the majestic Royal Palace remains as a tribute to the city's regal legacy. Stockholm's culture is a tapestry rich in Nobel Prize legacies, a lasting literary legacy, and a lively art scene, all of which coexist with cutting-edge fashion and pioneering culinary trends.

Immerse yourself in the city's vivid history at the Vasa Museum, where you may marvel at an almost entirely intact 17th-century ship, or lose yourself in Sweden's past at the Skansen Open-Air Museum. As you walk around the city, you'll feel the warmth of "Fika" - the beloved Swedish coffee break - and maybe even the beautiful notes of ABBA, which reflect the essence of Stockholm's love of music.

Stockholm's cultural fabric is intertwined with its love of the environment, as seen by the perfectly maintained green spaces and pure seas that lap the city's countless ports. As Stockholm continues to lead as a Green Capital, you are invited to explore, connect with, and enjoy Stockholm - a city that lives in harmony with its history and future. Welcome, and let the enchantment of this Nordic treasure enchant you.

The Top 7 Reasons to Visit Stockholm!

Looking for a place to visit on your next city break? Have you ever considered traveling north? Here are the top seven reasons why you should choose Stockholm for your next city break!

1. Historical Context

There are several ancient buildings and museums to see in Stockholm, but the Vasa Museum is the city's most popular tourist destination. Dedicated to a mostly undamaged Swedish vessel built under the instructions of King Gustavus Adolphus of Sweden, which sank during its first voyage in 1628. She was the biggest ship of her period, and after being lost to time after her bronze cannons were removed, she remained in relatively excellent condition until being towed out of the busy shipping path where she was rediscovered in 1961. She represents Sweden's Great Power Period and is a national icon.

2. Clothes

Forget Ikea for a while; if you're interested in fashion and design, Stockholm is the place to go to watch the latest trends hit the storefronts and streets! From shabby chic cafés attracting hipsters with their long skinny lattes to high-street home ware stores brimming with gorgeous products ready to equip your home, there's something for everyone. The impact of other regions of Europe is visible in the blue-haired teenagers evocative of Berlin, a common hair color among the city's younger people.

3. Natural Radiance

Northern Europe is highly recognized for its natural beauty, particularly in the fjords and lakes that make up these nations. Stockholm may not be at the center of this wild region, but it has subtle natural accents interwoven throughout the city. The Stockholm Harbor, the numerous trees lining the streets, or the parks and gardens might all be examples. The Kungsträdgrden, or Kings Garden, is a local and tourist favorite located north of the Parliament House and The Royal Palace. This is an open space with street cafés, food sellers, and park seats, but the cherry blossom strip attracts people here. If you visit in the spring, the brilliant pink flowers that cover the metropolitan backdrop will not disappoint.

4. Eating

Sweden isn't famed for its culinary prowess, with boiled fish and potatoes being a popular Northern European meal. Having said that, there is a lot more to the city than preconceptions and typical rural fare. Reindeer steak with "pink in the middle" mashed sweet potato that melts on your tongue, a must-try that will set you back a few krona but is well worth it! If you book a bed and breakfast in Stockholm, you will be able to sample local dishes.

There are also several sushi restaurants and vegetarian cafes, and practically any convenience shop will sell you a hot dog on the go! (A common guilty pleasure in Northern Europe!)

5. Bicycling

If you like cycling, a lot is going on in terms of bicycle infrastructure in most Northern cities. Sweden is no different. Bike banks are popular, and dedicated cycling lanes snake through the streets! If you need to rent equipment or have your own equipment serviced, a few outlets are dispersed about the city. You may also receive maps and information about a handful of the city's numerous cycling tours that take you to all the must-see spots! Some even include ferry rides so you can easily move around the waterfront. If you don't want to drive this time, that's fine too; there's a well-connected metro, and most tourist attractions are within walking distance if you stay downtown. Pedestrians, remember to look both ways for approaching motorcycles!

6. Architecture

Stockholm has no shortage of great structures, particularly in Gamla Stan, Stockholm's Old Town. A tiny island in Stockholm's harbor with narrow meandering alleyways, small boutique stores, and neighborhood cafés. It's really clean, and it has a magical air about it that makes you want to roam around and get lost in the murmur of the throng. The Royal Palace and Parliament House are located to the north of Gamla Stan and are an excellent place to begin. As you cross the port into the island, you will pass under massive archways with lion sculptures gazing over you.

7. The Language

Have you ever wanted to learn a new language but couldn't pick which one to study? Or are you too afraid to try? Why not learn Swedish? Because it has significantly fewer words than English, one word in Swedish may encompass five or 10 words in English. The majority of individuals here speaks excellent English and would gladly let you practice your Swenglish. If the worst happens, you can always switch back to English. However, it adds to the thrill if you try something new and exotic while traveling abroad! Also, maybe the next time you go to Ikea, you'll comprehend what the label says.

CHAPTER ONE

Travel Advice for Visiting Stockholm

Are you debating whether to spend cash or endure it all at the sauna? When visiting a city like Stockholm, you may plan every minute of every day and still be taken off guard by one tiny little item. Tickets for the train. Cash only. That kind of thing. You could even get caught in an embarrassing international gaffe, such as ordering a coffee at the incorrect time. In any case, this is as true in Scandinavia's cool capital as it is anyplace else. Want to know which stations to avoid and when to eat cake? Do you strip naked in a sauna or keep your clothes on? From metro tickets to greetings, here's everything you need to know for your first trip to Stockholm.

1. Sneaky Access to the Airport

Many visitors are unaware that, in addition to the pricey fast train and coaches, you may use public transportation from Arlanda airport to the city center. At either terminal, follow the signs to the local buses and search for the one that goes to Märsta station, which is on a commuter rail line. The entire ride to central Stockholm may be covered by a single ticket purchased using the SL app.

2. Don't Bring A Lot Of Money.

Stockholm plans to become a cashless city in the coming years, and many cafés, restaurants, and hotels have already implemented this concept. So, carry your bank card and only use cash if necessary on your vacation.

3. Look Outside Of the Metro Lines

It might be difficult to find suitable lodgings in Stockholm. Which is the finest island? What should you spend? And, maybe most importantly, can they all be conveniently accessed? The answer is yes in the inner city. But it's also worth goingfurther afield: accommodation prices fall when you seek along commuter train lines rather than simply metro lines. Don't be afraid of these local lines; they'll frequently deliver you just as fast to the city center!

4. Stay Away From the 'Stress Tunnel' Near Centralen

An early sunset usually tempts Stockholmers to leave the workplace at about 4 pm; therefore this is our rush hour for most of the year. If possible, avoid the central station, 'T-Centralen,' around 4 p.m. and around 8 a.m.—this is when the ' stress tunnel' connecting the different metro lines is at its busiest.

5. Breakfast On Weekdays Is Easy And Healthful.

In the morning, you'll typically find muesli and yogurt or bread rolls with ham and cheese served at cafés. On weekends, however, things are a little different. Popular brunch locations like Kitchen & Table and Greasy Spoon book up quickly, so get a reservation!

6. Bring Your Hardest Boots.

Bring some durable shoes if you're going on a winter trip. From November to March, the ground will be coated in 'slask,' a filthy mixture of melting snow and grit. It saves you from tripping, but it will leave a stain on your shoes!

7. Hold an Entire Swedish Conversation with Only Two Words

Swedes are well-known for their English abilities; in Stockholm, you'll hear and see English everywhere. Still, if you want to practice your Swedish, you may do so with little effort. You may say hello or farewell with 'hej' or 'hej hej' (the 'j' sounds like an English 'y'), and 'tack' indicates both thank you and please, making it extra simple to be courteous.

8. The Fika Taste

'Fika' is the Swedish coffee and cake ritual, which means that the city's top cafés will be packed in the afternoons, especially on weekends. The traditional fika is served with a cinnamon bun, but some cafes make their variations, such as the rhubarb crumble buns at Fabrique or the pistachio and blackcurrant version at Il Caffe. It's a packed time, but it's worth the effort.

9. Saunas Are Used To Expose Everything.

Another Nordic tradition is nakedness in the sauna. It's often preferred in Swedish culture to keep things private—except in the sauna. Expect to pack nothing except yourself and a towel, which will be used largely to dry oneself off after plunging into an icy-cold lake.

10. Set Aside A Clean-Eating Week for Stockholm.

This city's vegan options are unrivaled. Most cafés serve coffee with oat, almond, or soya milk, and you can buy great vegan ice cream in supermarkets or at Stikki Nikki.

You can also have vegan pulled pork (called oomph) at Max Burger, Vigrda, and many other burger joints.

11. Go To A Gallery Late At Night.

Thank god for Fotografiska, the photographic exhibition on Södermalm's northern shore, if you're a night owl seeking for something more intellectually engaging than a night on the tiles. This old factory remains open until 11 p.m. once the galleries have closed for business.

12. Lunch In Sweden Begins Early.

Lunch is the most important meal of the day in Sweden. Restaurants often serve buffet meals for a set charge and begin serving at noon. Oh, and sweets aren't usually served, but you can satisfy your sweet desire afterward!

13. Summertime Relaxation

Swedes take their vacations extremely seriously, usually by retreating to their rural homes or archipelago island getaways. This means that Stockholm is a bit of a ghost town during certain periods of the year, particularly after Midsummer in June and July. On the bright side, visitors get the entire city to themselves!

14. Island-Hop in Style at No Additional Cost

Your SL card (the Stockholm transit system) will allow you to board almost any mode of transportation, including some of the boats that sail between the inner-city islands. You may even use an SL ticket on boats to the archipelago during the winter season.

15. It's A Little Difficult To Get Booze Here... Systematic

The Swedish government holds an alcohol monopoly—at least, if it contains more than 3.5% ABV. For the strong stuff, go to the government-owned Systembolaget, which closes in the early afternoons on Saturdays and is closed on Sundays. If you want a 2% beer (affectionately called folköl, or 'the people's beer' by locals), you may find these at any conventional store.

16 Obtain A Pint At 4 p.m.

Rush hour also marks the beginning of 'After-Work,' a Swedish variant of happy hour that begins about 4:30 pm. Many pubs will sell a cheaper pint during these hours, and there's even a club called Out of Office that starts in the late afternoon rather than the late evening to accommodate thirsty office workers. Get your free entry ticket by downloading the club's app and dancing your suit off.

17. Culture without The Cost Of Admission

If beer and sauna culture aren't your thing, you can spend your Tuesday afternoon for free at a museum. The Nordic Museum is free on Wednesdays from 5-8 pm, while the Nobel Prize Museum is free on Tuesdays from 5-8 pm. Meanwhile, the Modern Art Museum in Skeppsholmen is open every day of the week.

18. The Two Words Needed For a Cheap Pint

Stockholmers are passionate beer fans, as seen by the city's numerous outstanding microbreweries and craft beer bars. That's not to suggest your pint has to be fancy or costly; at any establishment, you may get their lowest pint of beer by simply asking for a 'Stor Stark.'

19. In the Summer, Drink in The Evening Sunshine.

Summer drinking takes place outside. Bars may be found in a variety of unconventional outdoor places, including beneath a bridge: Trädgrden (the garden) opens at the end of May under Skanstull Bridge. As an added benefit, if you arrive before 7 p.m., you will escape any free admission and will be offered discounted drink bargains.

20. Plan Ahead Of Time to Avoid Cabs.

Taxis in Stockholm are quite pricey. Especially boat taxis (yes, really!) that will come and fetch you if you are trapped on an archipelago island. Check the SL app for the best travel alternatives ahead of time. The metro operates all night on weekends, but after 1 a.m. on weekdays, a night bus may be your best choice.

Stockholm Etiquette - What to Do and What Not to Do in Stockholm

Etiquette Fundamentals

- Much of Swedish etiquette is built on ensuring equality throughout exchanges. For example, praising individuals for their efforts and returning to frequent activities.

- When waiting to be served, everyone is required to create an orderly queue. There is hardly any need to get in front of those who came before you. In reality, many establishments employ a "queuing ticket" system, in which you obtain a number from a machine when you first enter the business. It is your turn to be served when your number is called.

- When someone answers the phone, they say 'Hall' ('Hello') and identify themselves.

- In Sweden, punctuality is vital. Avoid coming too early or too late for a meeting or event. If visitors come early, it is fairly unusual for them to sit in their car or walk around the block until the stated start time arrives.

Visiting

- It is customary for people to gather for 'fika'. Fika is similar to morning or afternoon tea in that it consists of coffee, tea, or soft drinks that are frequently accompanied by a small snack (such as a sandwich or pastry). People may gather for fika at cafés or at their homes.

- When visiting one another, arrangements are frequently made. Unannounced visits are rare.

- Guests are required to come at the time specified.

- Typically, people remove their shoes before entering someone's home, especially in the cold.

- If it's their first time coming, many Swedes will give them a comprehensive tour of the house.

- Typically, hosts will give their visitors a beverage, generally black coffee.

- It is courteous to depart immediately after finishing your meal. Guests are expected to stick around for coffee and discussion.

- Guests should thank their hosts for their hospitality the next time they meet. This is accomplished by saying "Tack för senast" (Thank you for the previous time).

Eating

- When completed eating, a person sets the utensils side by side on the plate.

- It is rude to leave any food on the plate.

- Typically, guests will wait for the host to give a second helping. It is not disrespectful to reject, and visitors are welcome to take extra if desired.

- Following the lunch, each guest will individually thank the host.

- When toasting one another, people look one another in the eyes.

- Some Swedes may offer each guest seven different varieties of cookies to taste. If you and your other visitors are provided a choice of cookies, it is critical that you only take one of each flavor.

Gifts

- Swedes unwrap gifts as soon as they receive them.

- It is customary for individuals to send presents for any youngsters who may be visiting the household.

What to Do and What Not to Do

Do's

- Be mindful of personal space. Maintain a bit more than an arm's length space and limit touching throughout a talk. Invading your Swedish counterpart's personal space may make them uncomfortable.

- If the chance comes, try to engage in 'fika' (coffee/tea, light snacks, and chat). Many Swedes love fika both at work and in their daily lives.

- Hold a discourse about nature. Swedes are proud of their natural environments, and many prefer spending time outside.

- Be on time for all appointments. Swedes place a great priority on being on time for any appointment (not too early, nor too late). Please notify your Swedish equivalent if you will be late.

- Try to keep your surroundings tidy, since Swedes feel it demonstrates a sense of respect for others. Avoid, for example, littering, entering someone's home without taking off your shoes, or spitting in public.

Don'ts

- Do not overstate or brag about your accomplishments. The Swedes admire humility.

- Avoid making jokes or using generalizations about various nationalities or cultures. This will almost certainly be received with disfavor.

- Be aware that your Swedish counterpart may become irritated or exasperated if you use loud voices or overly active body language.

- Use caution while addressing the arrival and settlement of refugees and migrants in Sweden, and keep in mind that you may not be able to assume someone's viewpoint or level of expertise on the subject. Avoid drawing parallels with migration in Australia since it occurs in a different context and magnitude.

- Avoid making people-to-people analogies between Sweden and the other Nordic nations (Denmark, Norway, Finland, and Iceland).

Greetings

- In Sweden, the most frequent greeting is a handshake. It is generally forceful and includes direct eye contact.

- When entering or departing a social gathering, most people will shake hands with everyone present.

- Handshakes are not as popular in rural places on a casual basis. Rather, it is connected with signing contracts, settling problems, or greeting in more official situations.

- If persons are far apart, they can welcome one another by nodding or raising their hands.

- When welcoming one another, friends and relatives will frequently embrace.

- A half-hug with a gentle backslap is frequent amongst males who are close and have not seen each other in a long time.

- People usually refer to one another by their first names. Titles are only used in formal contexts.

- A casual 'Hej' ('Hi') is the most frequently spoken greeting.

- The term 'Hej d' is commonly used to say farewell.

15 Things to Do and See in Stockholm

Discover one of Europe's best-preserved medieval cities, massive palaces, and a plethora of fascinating museums sprawled among 14 beautiful islands. Welcome to Stockholm, the captivating and stylish capital of Sweden. Whether you're in Stockholm for a Swedish honeymoon, a city break, or a Scandinavian road trip, there's plenty to do. It's a peaceful and lovely capital city with a surprising combination of cultural attractions, outdoor activities, and delicious food.

1. Admire the lovely Gamla Stan.

When visiting Stockholm, you'll most likely start in the city center. Gamla Stan, Stockholm's lovely Old Town. You'll fall in love with its immaculate cobblestone streets and colorful houses. The lively Stortorget plaza is a feature of this fairy-tale quarter, ideal for a drink or simply watching people go by. Explore the charming pedestrian zed roads beyond the main plaza to discover a plethora of great pubs, cafés, and stores, as well as much more.

Of course, Gamla Stan is home to several of Stockholm's most popular tourist sites, including the Royal Palace and the Stockholm Cathedral.

2. Djurgården Is Home To World-Class Museums.

One of the most popular islands in Stockholm is Djurgården. It is a big area of Stockholm's Royal National City Park, where locals go to unwind among the numerous forests and meadows. The island's extraordinary assortment of museums is the island's largest appeal for city tourists. There truly is something for everyone. ABBA the Museum, for example, chronicles the career of Sweden's most famous musical export. You'll be able to dress up like ABBA, sing along, and compose your song here.

Alternatively, the Nordic Museum transports you to the very beginnings of Swedish history. Skansen, an open-air museum that displays exhibits about Sweden's traditional people and ways of life, is another option. Don't miss the Vasa Museum, which is one of the most popular museums in Scandinavia (Denmark, Norway, and Sweden). It is the sole remaining 17th-century boat in the world, which drowned in Stockholm harbor on its inaugural trip in 1628. It's a significant, physical piece of history.

3. Discover Stockholm's Waterways.

You may have heard the Swedish capital referred to as the "Venice of the North" due to its numerous rivers and magnificent early modern architecture. However, the parallels end there, and Stockholm's moniker does not do credit to the city's bond with the sea that surrounds it. The Stockholm archipelago spans 80 kilometers (50 miles) and approximately 30,000 islands, separated by waterways navigable by boat. These range from tiny uninhabited islets to well-developed and popular tourist destinations. A trip to the city would be incomplete without a trip on the water. It may be one of the most romantic activities in Stockholm.

4. Swim at Lake Mälaren.

Why not continue your voyage on Stockholm's seas by visiting Lake Mälaren, Sweden's third-largest freshwater lake? Its easternmost bays are located on the city's outskirts and are easily accessible from the center. Lake Mälaren is the finest spot to swim if the city's waters lure you. Summertime will bring lots of visitors. Indeed, Stockholmers have been swimming here for generations, and the city's mild summers make a dip particularly appealing. If not, Lake Mälaren provides opportunities for animal viewing and picturesque hikes. It's well worth the drive out of town.

5. Get Lost In The Sprawling Royal Palace.

Back on dry ground, the Royal Palace in Gamla Stan is one of the most intriguing places to spend a day in Stockholm. This 18th-century structure, which is now the official house of the Swedish royal family, is one of Stockholm's most visited attractions. The Royal Palace is also one of Europe's biggest, with over 600 rooms. However, the King of Sweden still works here, so you won't be able to see them all. Nonetheless, there is a lot to see and do at the Palace. The Royal Apartments, for example, provide an insight into the daily lives of Scandinavian royalty. The Museum of Antiquities, meanwhile, is well-known for its collection of 17th-century Italian sculpture.

6. Gröna Lund Amusement Park Invites You To Join In The Fun.

We mentioned that Djurgården had something for everyone. Gröna Lund, the island's famous amusement park, is a wonderful way to spend an afternoon for families on vacation in Sweden and the young at heart. Gröna Lund's location in the city center makes it smaller than other theme parks. Despite its small size, it offers a diverse assortment of attractions, from exhilarating to family-friendly.

Evening performances by international musical acts are available. Seeing a show beneath Stockholm's lengthy sunsets may be one of the nicest things to do at night in Stockholm!

7. The Nobel Prize Museum Exhibits The History Of Brilliance.

Sweden is the home of the Nobel Prize, which is awarded annually to some of the finest minds in literature, science, and other fields. There are plenty of wonderful things to see if you're interested in the history and winners of the award - and even if you didn't think you were interested. Of course, the Nobel Prize Museum is an excellent place to begin. Its permanent displays tell a significant tale about the evolution of creativity. You may also enjoy guided tours, DJ performances, and events hosted by Nobel laureates.

8. Relax At One Of Stockholm's Spas.

A spa visit is one of the nicest things to do in Stockholm as a couple. You'll be spoiled with choices with so many wonderful alternatives available around the city. Centralbadet, located in the middle of Gamla Stan, is an excellent choice for visitors.

A classic Nordic sauna, an amazing swimming pool, and everything you'll need to pass away the afternoon can be found in a 1904 structure. Alternatively, explore the Hellasgrden Park and lake to the southwest of the city. Stockholm residents gather here to cool down in the ice pool before heading to the adjoining sauna.

9. Try Some Traditional Swedish Cuisine.

Scandinavian food is becoming increasingly popular in trendy restaurants throughout the world. Stockholm, however, is one of the greatest places to experience it in all its magnificence. Visit the city's food courts to try the pastries, candies, meats, and drinks available. To the north of Gamla Stan, for example, lies the Stermalm Market Hall, a Stockholm institution. Alternatively, in the summer, modern street food vendors line the river at Hornstulls Marknad. Of course, sample typical Swedish foods like Swedish meatballs (köttbullar), fried or cured fish, and reindeer while you're in town. They may be found at several of Gamla Stan's classic restaurants.

10. Take A Stroll In Södermalm.

If you're looking for genuinely great things to do in Stockholm, head to Södermalm - or just Söder, as the locals call it. It's a fashionable neighborhood recognized for its cool and laidback vibe, as well as its creative and stylish population. Explore vintage shops and boutiques, coffee shops and galleries, and late-night pubs. There's nothing better for a midday walk. Södermalm is also home to some of the nicest vistas of the city. Skinnarviksberget, for example, is Stockholm's highest peak.

11. Fotografiska Is A Photographic Museum In Stockholm.

Fotografiska, Stockholm's renowned photography museum, is a genuinely unmissable attraction in Södermalm. Fotografiska, like everything else in this unexpected region, is not your typical gallery space. This implies that there will be no permanent exhibits or artwork for sale. Fotografiska's work, on the other hand, attempts to inspire a better world via the art of photography. As a result, the emphasis is on the experience, which includes political exhibitions, events, exquisite eating, and more. Fotografiska, unsurprisingly, also features one of the trendiest bars in town.

12. Take The Metro.

It may not sound like a place to visit. However, Stockholm's enormous metro system is more than just a transportation system. It's a one-of-a-kind art exhibition worth seeing on its own. Traveling through Stockholm's metro system can expose you to a variety of surprises. Over 150 different local artisans adorned each station with artworks, sculptures, rock formations, and mosaics. It's a significant aspect of Stockholm's culture and a monument to the city's citizens' inventiveness. Try out the blue line for some of the more interesting performances.

13. Attend A Performance At The Royal Swedish Opera.

A visit to the Royal Swedish Opera may be the solution if you're seeking stylish things to do in Stockholm at night. This is the home of elegance, high culture, and real talent, located across the lake from the Royal Palace in an 18th-century opera theater. Whether you're looking for ballet, opera, or a strong symphony, you'll find it on this program. Winter is a great season to see a show. In the summer, you might be able to witness the Royal Swedish Ballet perform in Vitabergsparken, a public park in Södermalm.

14. Climb the City Hall tower in Stockholm.

The Stockholm City Hall is one of the most distinctive aspects of the city's skyline, with its strong red-brick façade and famous tower. It is essentially an official structure that hosts political and cultural activities. A glance inside results in a satisfying visit. You may, for example, witness the hall that holds the Nobel dinner, when the world's best brains are honored. The tower itself is the focal point of City Hall. Climb to the summit to see Sweden's national coat of arms' three crowns. It's a breathtaking perspective of the city.

15. Relax with Fika.

Finally, a vacation to Sweden would be incomplete without experiencing one of the country's most beloved traditions: fika. Fika is the simple act of stopping for a cup of coffee (or kaffi in Swedish) and a snack. Nonetheless, the Swedes have elevated this rite to the level of an art form. Fika isn't only a means of passing the time. Rather, it's time to mingle, catch up with friends, and unwind. Fika may be had at any café in Stockholm, including Gamla Stan and Södermalm.

Must-See Parks & Gardens in Stockholm

Stockholm is a green city where you can simply catch some fresh air, participate in sports, or engage in other outdoor activities. Parks and gardens may be found around the city. Some are natural bubbles on the city's fringes. Others are more planted and provide a spectacular location for picnics or breaks throughout your visit.

Most of them have sports fields, playgrounds, or recreation spaces. We look at the most stunning green spots in and around Stockholm.

Public Gardens in Gamla Stan

Gamla Stan is the district that corresponds to Stockholm's historic medieval city. It is a highly urbanized and densely built-up region. Nonetheless, there are some gardens there. They are quite organized, located in the center of historic buildings, with magnificent walks and lawns bordered by trees. These are manicured spaces that provide a really beautiful environment for a grass picnic in the center of town. Here are the Gamla Stan public gardens at your disposal:

- Riksplan Park is next to the Museum of Medieval Stockholm.

- Riddarhuset Palace's garden has an important historical aspect.

- Jünotappan Garden includes a good playground for children.

In the Norrmalm center

North of Gamla Stan, in Norrmalm City's business center, you may take a quiet break and fill up on greens in the middle of your shopping binge at the following gardens:

- Berzelii Park has a very classic structure: neatly maintained grass around a big monument intermingled with attractive tree-lined walks and chairs to sit on.

- Kungsträdgården Park is very lively. It offers a wide range of activities and events. In the winter, an ice rink is made up there.

- The Nora Bantorget garden is located at the western end of the area, near the banks of Klara Sjö. It's a wonderful, creative tiny garden.

In The Municipality Of Östermalm

The fashionable area of Östermalm, located right in the city center, is an important cultural hub in Stockholm. There are museums, cafés, and high-end boutiques, but there are also lovely gardens:

- The Humlegärden is a vast green space located between the Norrmalm and Östermalmdistricts. Large aisles enable jogging or running exercise. It has a playground, a skateboard ramp, and other amenities. It also serves as a library.

- The Gustaf Adolfsparken is a beautiful and peaceful park centered on a modest church. It's an excellent site in the middle of the city.

- Nobel Parken is a forested area on the water's edge. It is located at the end of Strandvägen Street, which runs along the harbor. It has little coves and beaches with wonderful views of the pier and pleasure boats.

The DjurgårdenIsland

A huge wooded area that extends from the Gardt residential zone to Alberget to the east of the city. It contains the island of Djurgården, which retains his name as well. It consists of many natural spaces:

- The Royal Urban National Park is a wonderful, heavily forested park. It feels extremely remote from Stockholm's inner metropolis, although it is very easy to get and very near to the city core. Long walks, treks, bike rides... are all options.

- The Garden of Rosendal is an exotic garden with a rustic feel. It consists of orchards, vegetable gardens, and meadows that are all in flower in the spring. It's crisscrossed with lovely walkways.

- The Frisens Park is a hill near the island's southern tip. You'll enjoy the constant dance of ferries and boats.

Island of Sodermalm

Södermalm Island is a big Stockholm island with various communities. The island's core is relatively developed; however, it is surrounded by parks. So you may enjoy some fresh air in the middle of nature without leaving fashionable districts.

- The Vitabergsparken in SoFo offers a panoramic view of the city. It's ideal for a picnic with a view of Stockholm.
- Tantolunden Park is most well-known for its sports fields and recreational amenities.

- Högalid Park is located on the island's east coast. It is built around a tiny church and includes a playground.

Island of Kungsholmen

Kungsholmen Island is one of Stockholm's biggest islands. It serves as a city district and is home to various communities. It is a more family-oriented and residential neighborhood with lovely green areas.

- Rambshov Park is a recreational area featuring sports fields, playgrounds, and big walks that wind through gorgeous lawns.

- Fredhällsparken is a lengthy park with shaded trails that is perfect for joggers.

- The Kronobergsparken is a popular family park due to its playgrounds and dog-friendly sections.

Island of Längholmen

The Vasterbrön Bridge connects the islands of Södermalm and Kungsholmen by passing through the island of Längholmen. It is a lush and well-preserved area. The island is mostly made up of a lovely park:

- Längholmsparken. This is its major draw, and it allows for a leisurely walk before arriving at the enormous island of Kungsholmen.

Outlying Regions to The North Of Stockholm

Two residential areas surround the city to the north. Vasa Park is well-known in Vasastan for its observatory, grass suited for picnics in the summer, and ice rink in the winter. The Karlbergs Slottspark is also nearby. This is Karlberg Palace's historical park. The wood, which faces the castle, is dotted with sports and recreational facilities. The Haga Park in Solna is located on the banks of Lake Brunnsviken, which is quite pleasant and refreshing in the summer.

Make the Most of Your Stockholm Summer

Stockholm is often regarded as one of the most beautiful places to visit in the summer, and there is no shortage of activities to do throughout the warmer months of the year. Enjoy famous outdoor attractions in and around Gamla Stan and the island of Djurgården, or travel out into the countryside and see the beautiful nature that surrounds the city. Visit the archipelago or one of the islands on Lake Mälaren, where you may see landmarks like Drottningholm Palace (Drottningholms slott) on Lovön Island or the Viking village of Birka on Björkö. The city also has plenty of peaceful outdoor places and urban swimming sites that are best experienced in the sun.

1. Discover the Archipelago

Travel from island to island by boat.

The Stockholm Archipelago is a collection of lovely islands just waiting to be discovered. There's a small-town idyll, an undisturbed environment, and little islands and skerries where others rarely set foot. Vaxholm has a historic stronghold called Vaxholm Castle, which is located on its island apart from the town. Set your eyes on the island of Möja and eat lunch in its delightful tiny guest house if you want to venture even further out to truly experience the archipelago calm.

2. Långholmen

Enjoy your summer independence with a refreshing plunge and fascinating history.

Långholmenis a city island where you may mix an invigorating swim with some historical attractions. Swimming is available on this island to the north of bigger Södermalm at either the sandy Lngholmsbadet or the craggier Lngholmens klippbad. Not far from these locations is one of Stockholm's former jails, which is now a museum where you can learn about life for the convicts who were detained here. If you're searching for a truly unique location to stay, you can even spend the night in one of the cells. They're a lot more inviting nowadays, as you could anticipate!

- **Open**: Lngholmen Prison Museum is open every day from 11 a.m. to 4 p.m. in Address: Långholmen Stockholm, Sweden.

3. Skansen

Step back in time to a bygone Sweden.

Skansen is an open-air museum where you may walk around and relive life in Sweden as it once was. The lush park is full of ancient structures from all around the country, and you'll even get to see and try out some of the handicrafts and daily activities that people used to perform hundreds of years ago. You may try your hand at glassblowing, among other things. The Skansen Aquarium and the Children's Zoo (Lill-Skansen) with all of its charming small creatures will especially appeal to younger visitors. Skansen is conveniently placed on the island of Djurgrden and is easily accessible by tram.

- **Address**: Djurgrdsslätten 49-51, Stockholm, Sweden (115 21).
- Open daily from 10 a.m. to 3 p.m.; guests may stay in the park for a few hours after it closes.

4. Djurgården

Stroll around the city's lush cultural island.

If you want to soak up some culture amid Stockholm's green lungs, Djurgården is the place to go. The world-famous Vasa Museum and the Nordic Museum (Nordiska Museet) may be found here, as well as many additional sites and attractions that not everyone is aware of. enjoy a journey to Rosendal Palace in the center of Djurgrden for a guided tour of the castle, or enjoy a stroll around the magnificent gardens next door. There are also lots of places in the vicinity to grab a cup of coffee or a bite to eat.

- **Place**: Djurgrden, Stockholm, Sweden
- **Open**: Always open; museum hours vary.

5. Fjällgatan

Fjällgatan is a street high up on the hills of Södermalm where you may wander past some of the island's oldest buildings, but it is arguably most known for the spectacular views from its observation platform. Views of the city and lake may be had before taking a stroll down to the Museum of Photography (Fotografiska) beside the quay, a few flights of steps below Fjällgatan. Then visit some of the independent boutique boutiques in Södermalm, or have lunch at one of the nearby restaurants. Slussen Station on the island of Södermalm is just a short walk away from Fjällgatan.

- **Address**: Fjällgatan in Stockholm, Sweden
- **Open**: Always available

6. Royal Guards Changing (Högvaktsavlösningen)

Witness an enduring and remarkable tradition.

The Changing of the Royal Guards (Högvaktsavlösningen) in Stockholm is a great experience and a daily chance to see Sweden and its monarchy in action. The Royal Guards of Stockholm Palace in Gamla Stan are part of a long-standing institution that dates back to the 16th century. The changing of the guard is a grandiose ceremony that begins with a procession on foot or horseback. The path to the palace changes depending on the season, and the ritual is accompanied by a marching band during the summer months. The much-loved ritual begins after everyone is in place in the outer courtyard. If you happen to be in Stockholm during a state visit, you will be able to witness an even statelier version of the ritual.

- **Location**: Slottsbacken 1, 111-30 Stockholm, Sweden

7. Kristineberg Golf Bar (Golfbaren Kristineberg)

Combine mini golf and a bar crawl.

The Golf Bar (Golfbaren Kristineberg) in Stockholm is the only venue in town where you can play mini golf while also going to the pub. The Golf Bar, located immediately near to Kristineberg Metro Station on the island of Kungsholmen, allows you to play mini-golf on courses created by a two-time world champion. If you're of legal drinking age, you may also have a glass of something sparkling while you play, while alcohol-free choices are also available for younger people.

- **Address**: Hjalmar Söderbergs väg 10, 112 52 Stockholm, Sweden
- Operating hours are seasonally dependent.
- **Phone**: +46 8 618 61 05 8.

8. Flea Market

Get a good deal at a summer market.

Summer is the ideal season to go treasure hunting among the stalls and merchants at one of Stockholm's many flea markets. Make like a true Stockholmer and come to Hågelby Park in the Tumba neighborhood for a massive vehicle boot sale. If you prefer to keep your bargain searching closer to the center, go to the Hornstull Market, which is held along the water's edge from early April to late September and is a terrific place to buy everything from ancient antiques to vintage clothes. Enjoy some excellent food from one of the numerous food trucks that usually park up for the event.

9. Tantostranden Beach.

Dive into an urban sanctuary.

Tantostranden Beach is a beautiful swimming destination in a convenient location, making it ideal for unwinding after a day of shopping or amusement in the city. The beach is located in the neighborhood of Hornstull on the island of Södermalm, making it ideal for a refreshing plunge after a stroll in the adjacent park, as well as a pleasant area to enjoy the summer heat with an ice cream in hand. If you visit after dark, you may enjoy your evening swim against a backdrop of lights from the new buildings on Liljeholm Quay to truly maximize the metropolitan sense.

- **Address**: Skarpskyttestigen 6, 117 41 Stockholm, Sweden • Hours of Operation: Always Open
- **Phone**: +46 8 508 12000

10. Ulriksdal Palace Park (Ulriksdals Slottspark)

Take in the beauty made by nature and man.

Ulriksdal Palace (Ulriksdals slott) is located in the Stockholm suburb of Solna and features a spectacular palace garden with baroque embellishments, romanticism, and neoclassical elegance. The park began its existence as a magnificent baroque garden, but it has since altered with the trends, with numerous remnants of the many styles present in the park today. There is an English garden in the Romantic style, for example, with modern classicism flourishes in the shape of the square water basin and its fountain. In addition to its floral splendor, the royal garden is home to several noble statues and some stunning buildings.

- **Address**: Slottsallén, 170 79 Solna, Sweden
- **Hours**: Always open
- **Phone**: +46 8 402 62 80

EXERCISE

Is Stockholm Worth Visiting with the above Reasons?

_____
_____
_____
_____
_____
_____
_____

Did you Learn Anything new with the Travel Advices, Etiquettes and What to do and What Not to Do?

_____
_____
_____
_____
_____
_____
_____
_____

How Do You Plan to Make the Most of your Trip to Stockholm with this Guide?

DID YOU SMILE TODAY?

49 | VISIT STOCKHOLM

CHAPTER TWO

Advice and Information on Travel Planning

Difference in Time

Sweden is an hour ahead of the UK and observes daylight saving time in the summer, so the time difference is always there.

Money

The Swedish Krona is the official currency, and it is split into 100 öre. Currency exchange is best done at currency exchange bureaus (in airports and major cities), banks, or post offices. Unlike currency exchanges, Swedish banks do not exchange traveler's checks. International credit cards are commonly accepted, and ATMs (bankomats) are available at most bank offices. Banks are open from 09:30 to 15:00 Monday through Friday (until 17:00 on Thursdays in general).

Electrical Power and Plugs

220 volts; European plug, so bring an adaptor for any UK equipment.

Local Attractions

Shops are generally open from 09:30 to 18:00 Monday through Friday and until 15:00 on Saturday. On Mondays, several museums are closed.

Media

The Swedes are voracious readers of newspapers. Aftonbladet (social democratic), Dagens Nyheter (liberal), and Svenska Dagbladet (conservative) are among the main titles. Sweden pioneered the free daily Metro. Foreign newspapers are also sold on newsstands (pressbyra).

Post

Post offices are few (open Monday through Friday from 9:00 a.m. to 6:00 p.m., and Saturdays from 9:00 a.m. to 1:00 p.m.). The majority of postal services are now provided by supermarkets, and certain tourist offices now sell stamps.

Phone

To call Sweden from the UK, add 00 46 to the beginning of the number you're calling (this removes the initial zero). To contact the UK from Sweden, dial 00 44 before the number (again, no first zero).

Internet and Cell Phone Coverage

Wi-Fi is commonly available, and cell phone service is adequate. Check with your operator for information on roaming rates and service conditions.

Currency

SEK

Visa and Passport Requirements

Visa Information for Sweden:

A visa is not required for British nationals to enter Sweden.

Passport Validity for Travel to Sweden:

For visits of up to three months, your passport should be valid for the period of your stay. Please get in touch with the embassy for more information.

Culture

Population (2023): 10,612,086

Swedish is the official language.

Language Used

Westrobothnian (from the coastal areas of Westrobothnia and Norrbotten); Dalecarlian (spoken primarily in the Älvdalen Municipality and other northern parts of the Dalarna province); Modern Gutnish (spoken in Gotland and Fårö); Jamtlandic (spoken primarily in Jämtland); and Scanian (spoken in Scania province) are some regional dialects. Finish, Meankieki, Tiddish, Sami (from the indigenous inhabitants of Lapland), and Romani are other minority languages. All around the nation, English is a commonly spoken language.

People

Minority groups such as Finns and Sami (Lapland natives) are included in the overall Swedish population. Immigrants make up somewhat more than 10% of the Swedish population.

Religion

Although many Swedes do not follow their religion, the Lutheran Church of Sweden has a strong moral effect on Swedish society. Catholics, Orthodox Christians, Jews, Muslims, and Buddhists share the remaining 20%.

National Holiday

The 6th of June marks the anniversary of Gustav Vasa 1's election (1523).

Schedule of Holidays

- January 1: New Year's Day (also a holiday on December 31).
- January 6th is Epiphany.
- Easter is celebrated from late March until early April.
- May is the month of Ascension and Pentecost.
- May 1st is Labor Day.
- June 6th is National Day.
- Summer Solstice event (last Saturday in June) (the Friday before a holiday).
- All Saints Day falls between October and November.
- December 13: St. Lucy's Day.
- Christmas Day is December 25 (the 24th and 26th are also holidays).

History

Although Sweden has been inhabited for thousands of years, notably by the indigenous Sami people of Lapland, the Viking period of Swedish history is an ideal place to begin when studying Swedish history. They had a spirit of adventure and a hunger for commerce and trade, so they traveled to the East and established trade lines to the Middle East through Russia and Ukraine. Christianity arrived in the nation in the 11th century, and Uppsala became the first Swedish diocese in 1164. The Church marks the beginning of clan union and the establishment of the foundations of a state.

There had been a few "kings" before, but there was no ideological glue to hold everyone together. With the support of the Swedish nobles, Queen Margaret I of Denmark unified the Nordic realms of Sweden, Denmark, and Norway in the Union of Kalmar in 1397, although this exacerbated difficulties with both Norway and Denmark. Gustav Vasa campaigned for an autonomous Sweden without the Union of Kalmar in the 16th century, and he also severed Sweden's links with the Catholic Church by creating the Swedish Lutheran Church.

Sweden obtained control of most of the Baltic area in the late 17th and early 18th centuries and achieved enormous strength, notably by controlling key exports like as grain, iron, copper, lumber, tar, hemp, and furs. Norway declared independence in 1814, prompting Sweden to form a personal union with it. The kingdom was handed to the Crown Prince of Sweden as part of a union that meant Sweden and Norway shared a similar monarch and foreign policy.

This lasted until the union was abolished in a vote in 1905. Sweden maintained political neutrality throughout the twentieth century, including throughout both World Wars. Sweden backed Finland during the Winter War (1939-1940), in which Finland fought the USSR, and stayed neutral throughout the Cold War. Sweden is no longer a member of any military alliance. It hosted the inaugural Earth Summit in Stockholm in 1972, and it has been a member of the European Union since 1995.

Policy

Sweden has a parliamentary system and is a constitutional monarchy. The monarch serves only as a representative. The parliament (Riksdag) comprises 349 members (40 percent of them are women) who are elected for four years. The Speaker of Parliament appoints the Minister of State (prime minister). The government and parliament collaborate to create legislation, with the Supreme Court presiding over the legal system.

Swedish Celebrities

- Kristina Vasa (1626-1689), Queen of Sweden, was recognized for her extravagance and extravagant spending, as well as her understanding of art and literature. Religion, philosophy, and mathematics are all disciplines. She deposed the crown in 1654, at the height of Sweden's glory, and converted to Catholicism.

- Björn Borg was born in 1956. This world-famous tennis player is regarded as one of the finest players in the sport's history.

Alfred Nobel was a scientist, inventor, businessman, and writer who lived from 1833 to 1896. He founded the Nobel Prize, which recognizes and celebrates persons who have made significant contributions to physics, chemistry, medicine, and literature, as well as those who struggle for peace. He developed dynamite and possessed 355 patents, and after his death, he gave a multi-million dollar wealth to the Nobel Prize organization.

- Ingmar Bergman (1918-2007), is regarded as one of cinema's great masters.

- Selma Lagerlof (1858-1940) was the first woman to earn the Nobel Prize in Literature (1909).

- ABBA (1970-1982): This Swedish pop group rose to prominence in the 1970s with their songs, and their music remains popular today. In Sweden's capital, Stockholm, there is a museum dedicated to the band and their music.

Etiquette

The Swedes are polite, courteous, and on time. Tipping is not requested; however, if you wish to give 10% as a token of your appreciation after a wonderful experience, the staff will welcome it.

Shopping

Traditional Swedish ornamental goods, especially Sami Lappish things, provide lovely gifts for others or keepsakes to remember your journey to Sweden. Whether you prefer wooden kitchenware, glass, porcelain, or ceramics, there will be a plethora of boutiques and artisan stores selling handcrafted products.

Food

Traditional Swedish cuisine is built around potatoes, pigs, and fish (particularly herring, cod, and salmon). There's also reindeer and other game, crabs, mushrooms, and, of course, meatballs (köttbullar). A simple dish of potatoes with poached salmon and dill sauce is a classic, but there's also herring terrine (strömmingslador), salmon pudding (laxpudding), ground apple butter cookies with fried bacon and cranberries (raggmunk), and rosehip soup served sweet and cold (nyponsoppa). The classic Smorgas is a slice of bread topped with shrimp, smoked salmon, herring, and cucumber slices, but many restaurants are making updated variations of these open sandwiches.

Restaurants occasionally serve smörgasbord buffets, which include a variety of smorgas. Breakfast is strong and filling to get you through the day; lunch is usually light; and the evening meal is eaten early, usually around 6 p.m. (restaurants normally do not serve after 9 p.m.). Fike is the act of taking a coffee or food break, which is usually done by candlelight. This is the Swedish version of afternoon tea, but it may happen whenever you choose.

Drink

The water from the tap is always pure and of high quality. Sweden has good beer as well, with four types: Lättöl (lower alcohol), Folköl, Mellanöl, and Starköl (the latter being the most frequent in pubs). Brandy is the traditional drink to accompany herring, and tastes range from classic to trendy. Mulled wine is accessible around Christmas as a delightful, spicy, warming drink throughout the chilly months.

Travel Essentials and Tips for Stockholm

If you prefer historical monuments, natural beauty, and a mix of urban and rural experiences, Stockholm should be your next vacation. And if you're wondering what to bring for a trip to Stockholm for the first time, keep reading. The Swedish capital is famed for its gorgeous architecture, picturesque canals, and rich cultural legacy, and it is one of Europe's most intriguing cities. Whether you're searching for adventure, history, or a quiet getaway, it promises to be a memorable experience packed with memories to last a lifetime.

Stockholm Travel Essentials

Before you prepare your vacation and packing list for Stockholm, consider the time of year you'll be visiting. Summer, from June to August, is the finest time to come since it has the hottest temperatures and the longest daylight hours, making it ideal for outdoor activities or island hopping around the archipelago. The Swedish capital is also worth seeing in the winter. Despite the cold weather, the city entices visitors with a magnificent winter wonderland, stunning scenery, and a festive mood.

In adjacent parks and woods, visitors may enjoy a variety of winter sports such as ice skating, skiing, and snowshoeing. Even in the summer, temperatures might dip in the evening, so bring a light jacket or sweater. Because the weather may be unexpected, it's always a good idea to be prepared for all four seasons. Without further ado, these are the items you should bring:

Summer:

- Lightweight clothing options include cotton or linen shirts, shorts, and skirts.
- A lightweight jacket
- Sweater for cool nights
- Sunglasses
- Eyeglasses
- Walking boots with minimal weight
- A sunscreen
- Water container that may be reused

Fall:

- Clothing that is layered
- A light sweater
- A jacket
- Waterproof jacket
- An umbrella
- Sturdy walking shoes
- Scarf
- Hat

Winter:

- Thermal attire
- The use of layers
- A winter hat
- Protective gloves

- Scarf
- Waterproof footwear
- Cozy socks

Spring:

- The use of layers
- Waterproof jacket
- Fashionable hoodies
- An umbrella
- Sturdy walking shoes
- Trousers
- Scarf
- Hat

Other Things to Bring on Vacation

- Valid ID / Passport
- Travel protection insurance
- Digital camera
- Laptop and related items
- Scarf with several uses
- A flashlight
- Daypack
- Personal care products
- Adapter for travel

What to Wear in Stockholm - Clothing Styling Tips & More

- Stockholm is well-known for its fashion-conscious residents. Dressing smartly for them is balancing comfort and grace. And you should do the same.

- Wear monochromatic clothes - Swedes keep their fashion basic and stylish. Choose pieces that are basic and timeless in neutral hues such as black, white, gray, and beige.

- Select natural textiles - Choose clothing made of natural, pleasant materials such as wool, linen, or cotton.

- Layer - wear lightweight pieces that can be removed or added quickly, such as a sweater over a shirt or a scarf over a coat.

- Dress formally for the eateries.

- Accessorize - add a personal touch to your ensembles by wearing scarves, hats, and jewelry.

- Carry a backpack - The most practical accessory you can wear while in Stockholm is a sleek, multifunctional, and water-resistant backpack. If you simply want to travel with a carry-on, our Nordace Siena II Totepack is the perfect option. It has clever compartments and lots of room for all your belongings. And because it can be worn as a backpack or tote, it can go with every clothing and scenario.

Pack your bags and set out toward the country of the midnight sun!

When Is the Best Time to Visit Stockholm?

Stockholm, the self-proclaimed capital of Scandinavia, is Sweden's largest city and capital. It takes pride in being an open city that accepts new ideas and viewpoints, as well as a bustling destination brimming with advances not just in technology but also in music, design, and fashion. It is spread across 14 islands and is jam-packed with activities, historical sights, museums, top-rated restaurants, and a thriving nightlife scene. So the ideal time to visit Stockholm depends on what you want to do and see in such a lovely city.

Stockholm is open all year, allowing you to enjoy all four seasons, from a lengthy, snowy winter to a warm, pleasant summer. Summer is the busiest season, with extended daylight hours and ideal weather for walking tours, kayaking, biking throughout the city, and attending outdoor activities. If you want to avoid the crowds, visiting Stockholm during the off-season allows you to experience the city in a new light.

You won't have to worry about anything when getting lost in Stockholm if you've taken care of your baggage. June is the sunniest month in Stockholm, with roughly 10 hours of sunlight each day, while December has the shortest days. It receives 170 days of precipitation on average, with a combination of rain and snow, notably during the winter and fall months. The yearly average temperature in the city ranges from 22°F (-5.6°C) to 72°F (22.2°C). Temperatures seldom drop below 6°F (-14.4°C) in the winter and rarely exceed 81°F (27.2°C) in the summer.

Summer In Stockholm Lasts From June To August.

While most European cities melt in the hot summer heat, Stockholm has milder weather, allowing you to spend your days exploring urban nature. Its daily high temperatures range from 68°F (20°C) to 81°F (27.2°C), with an average low of 56°F (13.3°C). It's the sunniest season of the year, with the sun rising early and setting late at night. June and July have the highest UV index, and despite being one of the warmest months, July is the rainiest in Stockholm, with nine days of rain.

Summer is peak season in Stockholm, with many tourists enjoying festivals and open-air events and exploring the city's key attractions. Pack a pair of comfy walking shoes for exploring the great outdoors. To remain cool, pack shorts, t-shirts, sandals, skirts, or other light attire. Because it might get humid in Stockholm in July and August, pack a raincoat or umbrella.

Stockholm has water almost everywhere, and it's so clean and clear that anyone may swim in the heart of the city. In and around the city, you'll have no problem locating a beautiful beach to relax on. Bring your bathing suit or preferred beachwear even if you don't intend to swim. This is because you'll be enticed to dive into those crystal-clear waters and participate in some aquatic sports throughout the summer months.

Along with excellent summer weather, various tourist attractions and eateries operate throughout the city to welcome guests. Locals leave work as early as possible to spend their weekends hiking, sailing, or boating. With its combination of verdant islands and open water, Björnö nature reserve is a favorite site in the Stockholm archipelago for outdoor enthusiasts. With a nice woodland route, kayak rentals, and an underwater snorkel trail, it's a popular natural reserve, especially among swimmers and hikers.

When the temperature rises and the sun shines brilliantly in early June, there's perhaps no better way to enjoy smörgstrta than in its natural setting. To mix leisure and well-being with wonderful cuisine in green settings, visit a garden café like Äppelfabriken and sample a home-brewed beer. You may also go camping with your friends and family or by yourself to disconnect, recharge, and get away from the rush and commotion of the city.

One of the disadvantages of living in the city at this time of year is being unable to sleep. It's mostly due to the extended daylight hours during midsummer, with rising as early as 3:30 a.m. and sunset as late as 10 p.m. However, this means you'll have more time to spend exploring and taking advantage of the peak season. Just don't expect to have a certain location or activity all to yourself because summer in Stockholm is the biggest season, with large crowds and costly accommodation and hotel room costs.

Fall In Stockholm Lasts From September To November.

Many people believe that early fall is the greatest time to visit Stockholm because of the pleasant weather and softer light. The weather begins to cool, and daily temperatures fall from 65°F (18.3°C) to 38°F (3.3°C), seldom reaching 73°F (22.8°C) or falling below 29°F (-1.67°C). There will still be plenty of light between early September and early November, but the Swedish capital will also turn cold and comforting as the sun sets.

The likelihood of rain in Stockholm rises throughout the fall season, so pack an umbrella and waterproof shoes or boots. You'll also need a waterproof jacket and several warm sweaters, especially if you intend to walk around the parks and gardens. Layering is the key to being warm in the metropolis, as it is in other places, especially with its changeable fall weather. And when winter approaches, you'll need a hat, gloves, and a knit scarf.

Fall in Stockholm is a lovely season, as seen by its vibrant landscapes. As the seasons change, the color of the leaves will shift from yellow to golden and orange to red. The daylight hours shorten, crowds thin out during peak season, and only residents and a few guests enjoy the remaining rays of the warm summer sun.

Rooftop hiking and wild mushroom gathering are two of Stockholm's most popular fall pastimes. Of course, there are some Halloween activities that you should not miss. After the season, you'll also find Christmas markets open.

However, two of the city's longest-running cultural events, the Stockholm International Film Festival and the Stockholm Jazz Festival, take place around this time. The cinema festival showcases films from all over the world, whereas the jazz festival dates back to 1980, making it one of Sweden's oldest events.

Stockholm Half Marathon, an annual event conducted in September, is also taking place in the fall. It follows a simple route through numerous inner-city locations and concludes in front of the Royal Palace. The Stockholm Beer & Whisky Festival, founded in 1992, has been one of the worlds most prominent and largest beverage events. It usually begins between mid-September and early October.

Although fall is a low season with lower hotel rates, the events, especially the annual Stockholm Design Week, draw a diverse clientele. To minimize disappointment, get your tickets and book your flights and lodgings as soon as possible.

Winter In Stockholm Lasts From December To February.

Stockholm's winter is lengthy, chilly, and mainly gloomy. Although December is the first month of winter, it begins to snow and turn into a winter wonderland in early November or even late October. Temperatures can plummet to as low as 26.6°F (-3°C) by December and 30.2°F (-1°C) in January, the coldest month of the year. The city's typical winter temperature fluctuates between 23°F (-5°C) to 48.2°F (9°C), with fewer sunny days.

Don't overlook Stockholm's winter season. If you don't bundle up while exploring, you might not make it till the chill sets in. So stuff those additional layers of clothing into your bag before you go. Winter coats, jackets, a raincoat, plus hats, gloves, and scarves are all required.

If you visit Stockholm in the winter, you will notice that the days are shorter and darker, since the sun sets before 3 p.m. in December. The sun can also rise as late as 8:30 a.m. regularly. However, just because it appears gloomy and dismal doesn't imply you'll have a dull winter in Stockholm. Why should you be worried by a snowy winter day if Swedes like being outside? Make a thermos of coffee or hot chocolate for everyone and go on a winter expedition.

During the winter season, shopping is a popular pastime, especially at Christmas markets. Those booths brimming with boundless deliciousness may brighten the bleak winter days. Vendors provide delicious cuisine, high-quality handcrafted goods, and even entertaining activities. Skansen's Christmas Market, which goes back to 1903, is one of the country's largest and oldest Christmas markets.

The off-season, from December to February, is the greatest time to visit Stockholm for budget tourists. Winter in Stockholm may not be as active as summer or as colorful as fall, but it has its unique charm worth experiencing. Candles and Christmas lights illuminate the dreary days, while choirs perform throughout the city. You could even see the Northern Lights if you're lucky.

You may also participate in winter activities such as ice skating or cross-country skiing. Furthermore, hotels are substantially less expensive, travel discounts are frequently available, and you may have a room to yourself.

Spring In Stockholm Lasts From March Until May.

The weather in Stockholm changes during the spring as the temperature progressively rises. The days are still frigid and dismal, and snowfall is not uncommon. Snow might fall as late as March or early April. During the spring shoulder season, the temperature in the city fluctuates between 36.9°F (2.7°C) and 64.8°F (18.2°C), seldom reaching 73°F (22.8°C) or going below 25°F (-3.9°C).

The season is still in its early stages, but as the days grow longer, residents and visitors alike begin to plan for the summer celebrations. In May, the temperature will progressively climb, with an average high of 59°F (15°C) and a low of 42.8°F (6°C). Around this month, the Swedish capital will also experience an additional 17 hours of sunlight.

Winter coats and jackets will still be required at the start of spring, or until early April. As the temperature rises, you may begin to remove those heavyweight garments. Bring a suitable jacket and a pair of waterproof shoes or boots, especially if you want to go on outdoor hikes.

Bergius Botanic Garden on Lake Brunnsviken is a great place to observe beautiful blossoms.

It's a beautiful haven for nature lovers and plant aficionados. The lovely cherry blossoms may also be seen in Kungsträdgrden, a key park and plaza in downtown Stockholm. Djurgrden is another springtime attraction worth seeing. It's a central Stockholm island with greenhouses and orchards, as well as stunning shoreline bike and walking pathways.

If it's too cold outside in the spring, you may always explore the city's museums, galleries, palaces, and other cultural sites. Then, move from one restaurant to the next and enjoy the country's diverse cuisines and wonderful meals. If your appetite has been filled, Stockholm also boasts art exhibitions, theatrical improvements, and live music places worth seeing out in the frigid springtime.

When Is The Ideal Time For You To Visit Stockholm?

No matter what time of year you come, there are various ways to make the most of your stay in Stockholm. If you want to get the ultimate tourist experience, come during the busy summer months. It's the time of year when the city comes alive with outdoor events, open-air activities, beach fun, and celebrations.

Those who like the low season with fewer visitors, however, should come in winter or late fall. Aside from the Christmas markets and light displays that lend life and energy to the city, various theaters, ballets, museums, and indoor attractions open their doors to give the ideal getaway from the frigid weather.

Useful Phrases and Words for Travelers

Want to impress the locals with some common Stockholm phrases? Here's where to begin! Swedes are widely regarded as outstanding English speakers. In other words, travelers who do not speak Swedish will have little trouble navigating Stockholm. However, if you want to impress the locals, you should familiarize yourself with the local vernacular. Stockholm, like Skne County, Gotland, and the Gothenburg region, has its own distinct accent and lexicon. So, although "a fika and kanelbulle" elsewhere in Sweden implies a coffee with a lovely cinnamon bun, taking a "bulle" into town in Stockholm indicates something quite different.

Guide to Pronunciation

Some knowledge of a Scandinavian language is beneficial when trying to pronounce words in Swedish, and knowledge of German or Dutch can also aid with comprehending written Swedish. The vowels differ from those of English; yet, most consonants are pronounced similarly. Here are a few examples of exceptions.

Letter	Pronunciation in English
A	"aw" sound in claw
E	"e" sound in fell
I	"ee" sound in fleece
O	The pronunciation of "oo" in "moose" and "o" in

	"close" is similar.
U	"oo" sound in "moose"
Y	the pronunciation falls between that of "oo" in "moose" and "y" in "any" (the trick: shape your mouth as if you were going to say "y" but then try to say "oo")
Å	The pronunciation of "o" in "close" and "o" in "pot" is similar.
Ä	Pronounced like the "a" in "apple"
Ö	Pronounced like the "u" in "full"
J	"y" sound in yellow
G	Pronounced like the English "g" if it is followed by an a, o, or å; pronounced like the "y" in "yellow" if followed by an e, i, ä, or ö
K	Pronounced as "sh" if an e, i, ä, or ö follows; like the English letter "k" if an a, o, or å follows.
Rs	"sh" sound as in shop

Common Phrases and Greetings

When meeting and greeting Swedes for the first time, eye contact and a handshake are typically the standard. Hugs and kisses are normally reserved for close friends, and even then, public shows of love are usually kept to a minimum.

English Word/Phrase	Swedish Word/Phrase
Yes	Ja
No	Nej
Thank you	Tack
That's fine	Det är bra
You're welcome	Varsågod
Please	Snälla/Vänligen
Excuse me	Ursäkta mig/Förlåt
Hello	Hej
Goodbye	Adjö/Hej då
I do not understand	Jag förstår inte
Do you speak English?	Talar du engelska?
What is your name?	Vad heter du?
My name is...	Jag heter …

Getting Around Words

Except for the occasional deer or moose on the road, seeing Sweden by automobile is simple—the roads are well maintained and traffic jams are unusual. Taxis are pricey in comparison to other nations, thus taking public transit is frequently a better alternative.

There is a large train, coach, and bus network. Swebus Express is the country's largest bus operator, serving 150 locations around the country.

English Word/Phrase	Swedish Word/Phrase
Where is ...?	Var finns ...?
What time does the ... leave/arrive	Nar avgar/kommer?
Train	Tåget
Bus	Bussen
Boat	Båten
Tram	Spårvagnen
Tram stop	Spårvagnshållplatsen
Train station	Tågstationen
Bus stop	Busshållplatsen
Rooms available?	Lediga rum?
No vacancies	Fullt

Spending Money

If you want to carry a bit of Sweden home with you but are tired of the stereotypical wooden clogs and Viking helmet, several alternative goods scream "Sweden." Toy-sized wooden Dala horses, indigenous Sami handicrafts, and jewelry, such as reindeer leather bracelets and buttons fashioned from reindeer antlers, are among the items available.

English Word/Phrase	Swedish Word/Phrase
How much is it?	Hur mycket kostar den?
Zero	Noll
One	Ett
Two	Två
Three	Tre
Four	Fyra
Five	Fem
Six	Sex
Seven	Sju
Eight	Åtta
Nine	Nio
Ten	tio

Tourist Essentials

Outside of Stockholm, the Swedish archipelago consists of 24,000 islands, islets, and rocks; it is a summer paradise for city inhabitants. It is useful to know the names of facilities in and around towns when traveling throughout the nation.

English Word/Phrase	Swedish Word/Phrase
Tourist Information	Turistinformation
My hotel	Mitt hotel
Bank	Bank
Police Station	Polisstation
Post Office	Postkontoret
Embassy	Ambassaden
Public telephone	Offentlig telefon
Market	Marknaden
City center	Centrum
News agency	Nyhetsbyrå
Restrooms	Toalett
Entrance	Ingång
Exit	Utgång

Open	Öppen
Closed	Stängd
Men	Herrar
Women	Damer
What time does ... open/close?	När öppnar/stänger de?

Time of Day and Weekdays

Knowing your days of the week may be useful, especially when booking flights and hotels, organizing guided tours, or changing your schedule.

English Word/Phrase	Swedish Word/Phrase
Monday	Måndag
Tuesday	Tisdag
Wednesday	Onsdag
Thursday	Torsdag
Friday	Fredag
Saturday	Lördag
Sunday	Söndag
Today	Idag

Yesterday	Igår
Tomorrow	Imorgon
morning	Morgonen
Afternoon	Eftermiddagen
What time is it?	Vad ar klockan?

EXERCISE

How are the Travel Planning, Visa and Passport Requirements Helpful to you in your Planning Process?

_____
_____
_____
_____
_____
_____
_____
_____
_____
_____
_____
_____
_____
_____
_____

With The Travel Essentials and Tips, When Do You Think Is the Best Time for You to Visit Stockholm to Have the Most of Your Trip?

CHAPTER THREE

Best Places to Eat in Stockholm for Locals

Stockholm is a big city full of diverse restaurants and cafés, so knowing where the locals prefer to dine might be useful. With the inside scoop, y ou'll be able to taste the greatest, and sometimes most hidden, culinary delights the city has to offer. Choose from a simple burger in a casual setting to a fancy-tasting menu with drink pairings. Enjoy a nutritious bun or some traditional cold meats while listening to the swinging sounds of great jazz. Whether you're looking for a quick snack on the move or a complete evening of surprise and sensation, you'll quickly realize that excellent cuisine in Stockholm is serious business.

1. Vasastaden Lilla Ego

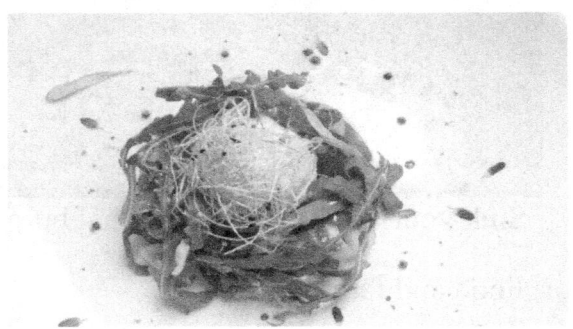

Fantastic cuisine served on weird wax tablecloths

Ideal for: Food and Couples

Lilla Ego, a critically acclaimed restaurant, is the ideal destination to please your taste buds without breaking the wallet.

Lilla Ego is in the Vasastaden area, slightly over a mile from Central Station and a few minutes' walk from the Odenplan Metro Station. Enjoy simple, uncomplicated Nordic meals alongside a well-picked assortment of beers, wines, and juices. Tables are issued a month in advance, and because the number of available places is limited and the restaurant is quite popular, it is best to reserve well in advance.

- **Address**: 69 Västmannagatan, 113 26 Stockholm, Sweden
- **Open**: Tuesday through Saturday, 5 p.m. to 11 p.m.
- **Phone**: +46 8 27 44 55

2. Vasastaden Flippin' Burgers

Sink your teeth into a traditional burger.

Ideal for: Food and families.

Flippin' Burgers is the place to go if you want high-quality homemade patties or vegetarian options without all the frills. The incredibly intimate establishment is located in the Vasastaden area, roughly a mile from Central Station. In a casual and inviting atmosphere, enjoy simply made but lovingly crafted burgers. There are also children's burgers and gluten-free baps, as well as thick, American-style milkshakes in a range of fascinating flavors. Although reservations are not available, many Stockholmers believe that their unrivaled burgers and the restaurant's emphasis on organic and local ingredients are well worth the short wait.

- **Address**: Observatoriegatan 8, Stockholm, Sweden (113 29).
- **Hours of operation**: Monday-Thursday 4 p.m. to 10 p.m., Friday: 11:00 a.m. to 10:00 p.m.; Saturday and Sunday: 12:00 p.m. to 10:00 p.m.

3. Östermalm Aubergine

In a truly local bar, you may sample a variety of cuisines.

Ideal for: Food and Couples

Aubergine is a cozy neighborhood tavern and a romantic venue in Stockholm for a memorable lunch or dinner. The restaurant is at the junction of Linnégatan and Jungfrugatan in the Östermalm neighborhood, about a 20-minute walk from Central Station. Enjoy a peaceful moment with your spouse or reserve a table for a bigger party. The menu changes with the seasons and places a strong emphasis on high-quality products.

Come in for a happy hour at the end of the day and enjoy the lively yet relaxed environment at the bar. The restaurant serves food à la carte and offers two budget-friendly specials each evening.

- **Location**: Linnégatan 38, 114 47 Stockholm, Sweden.
- **Hours of operation**: Monday-Thursday 11:30 a.m. to 11 p.m., 5 p.m. on Saturday and 11 a.m. to 1 a.m. on Friday
- **Phone**: +46 8 660 02 04

4. Östermalm saluhall (Östermalms market hall)

Östermalm Market Hall (Östermalms Saluhall) offers a wide variety of meats, seafood, wraps, and health items. The inexpensive food hall is located in Östermalm Square, which is only a 10-minute walk from Stockholm City or a 15-minute metro ride from T-Centralen Metro Station. Before taking up a chair at one of the eateries, hop from counter to counter and explore a world of flavors and delicacies. If you don't feel like eating a full dinner, simply taste all of the cheeses, breads, pastries, and confections on offer. There's also a wine bar where you can relax with a glass of red and watch the folks go by.

- **Address**: Östermalmstorg 114 39 Stockholm, Sweden
- **Hours of operation**: Monday-Friday 9:30 a.m.-7 p.m., Saturday 9:30 a.m.-5 p.m.

5. Södermalm ICHI

Discover Nordic cuisine made using Japanese methods.

Ideal for: Food, Couples, and Luxury

ICHI is a one-of-a-kind restaurant that serves Japanese twists on Western classics in the Yoshoku style of cuisine. Nordic and Japanese tastes take center stage, and because the menu changes according to fruit and season, there are new selections available virtually every day. ICHI is a short walk from Maria Square on Södermalm and roughly a ten-minute walk from the Medborgarplatsen Metro Station. Reservations can be made up to 60 days in advance and solely through their website. Allow enough time for your visit - a lunch at ICHI normally lasts 2 to 2.5 hours.

- **Address**: 38B Timmermansgatan, 118 55 Stockholm, Sweden
- **Hours of operation**: Wednesday-Saturday 5:30 p.m.-1 a.m.

6. Södermalm Punk Royale

Treat your taste buds to a fashionable and opulent gastronomic experience.

Ideal for: Food, Couples, and Luxury

Punk Royale is a rebellious yet elegant gastropub that serves a multi-course tasting menu with expertly curated beer pairings. The restaurant sits on Södermalm's island, slightly over a half mile from the Medborgarplatsen Metro Station. The wide menu is presented distinctively and amusingly, with an abundance of high-quality foods inventively displayed with plastic gloves, rat traps, and Lego bricks. The price is somewhat high, but it includes drink pairings, and the restaurant is so hip that it doesn't even disclose its opening hours on its website.

- **Address**: Folkungagatan 12B, Stockholm, Sweden (116 30).
- **Open Hour:** Tuesday-Saturday, 6 p.m.-midnight
- **Phone**: +46 72 938 12 84

7. The Swedish Army Museum (Armémuseum) has Artilleries.

Artilleries is a hidden gem where you may spend lunch or dinner in a contemporary, stylish setting under massive stone arches. The restaurant is located in Östermalm and may be reached by Artillerigatan or via the Swedish Army Museum across the courtyard from Riddargatan. The foods presented are Nordic classics with their distinct interpretation of European components. On a Tuesday evening, stop by for happy hour at the restaurant's friendly bar or to listen to live jazz. Four-legged guests are welcome, and there is even a dog menu!

- **Address**: 13 Artillerigatan, 114 51 Stockholm, Sweden
- **Hours of operation**: Tuesday-Thursday 11 a.m.-11 p.m., Friday-Saturday 11 a.m.-1 a.m.
- **Phone**: +46 8 664 34 30

8. Teatern Serves Elevated Street Food.

Teatern is the place to go for great street cuisine cooked by famous chefs in a relaxed atmosphere. The food court is located in the Ringen Mall, near the Skanstull Metro Station, at the junction of Götgatan and Ringvägen. Discover world-class hot dogs, veggie burgers, and delectable desserts of the finest caliber. There are tastes from Sweden and Italy, as well as India and Japan, all presented quickly, simply, and unpretentiously. Lunchtimes may be extremely busy, so arrive early if you want to ensure a table.

- **Address**: Götgatan 98, 11862 Stockholm, Sweden
- **Hours of operation**: Monday-Thursday 11 a.m.-9 p.m., Friday-Saturday 11 a.m.-10 p.m., and Sunday 11 a.m.-8 p.m

9. Norrmalm's Hötorgshallen

Hötorgshallen is home to approximately 40 different vendors and foods from all over the world, ensuring a one-of-a-kind gourmet experience. The contemporary food market is located in the downtown Stockholm suburb of Norrmalm, just a few minutes' walk from the downtown Station. Create your 3-course menu with tastes from across the world by choosing an appetizer, main dish, and dessert from various culinary traditions. Asian, Italian, and Spanish cuisines are just a few of the options available. Between courses, work up an appetite by wandering between vendors and sampling everything on offer.

- **Address**: 29 Sergelgatan, 111 57 Stockholm, Sweden
- **Hours of operation**: Monday through Thursday, 10 a.m. to 6 p.m., Friday, 10 a.m. to 7 p.m., and Saturday, 10 a.m.

10. Gamla Stan Cafés

Choose something sweet from a classic or trendy establishment.

Ideal for: Couples, Families, and Budget

Gamla stan's small cobblestone lanes are home to a diverse range of artisan bakeries, prominent confectioners, and sophisticated cafés, so a delightful treat is never far away. Gamla Stan, on the other side of the Vasa Bridge, is a quick 15-minute walk from Central Station. Fresh bread from the stone oven, traditional biscuits, and magnificent pastries are served alongside fair trade coffee, unusual teas, or steaming hot chocolate. Combine your coffee break with a visit to one of the art cafés in the district. Many also serve lighter lunch fare, and some even provide breakfast or afternoon tea. In the summer, you may relax on one of the terraces and enjoy your pastry while watching the throng.

Best Stockholm Foods for Everyone

In recent years, new Nordic and modern Swedish food has made waves, so why not sample some local cooking favorites while in the country's capital? Book a meal at a quaint small restaurant and learn how professional chefs have elevated traditional cuisine to new heights. If you're living in a self-catering apartment or hostel with a kitchen, why not try making something yourself? Purchase a classic cookbook from a bookstore, gather supplies from romantic market halls or the local square, and turn cooking into an activity you can do with your lover, family, or friends. After all, traditional Swedish cuisine is about more than simply nourishing and soothing flavors; it's also about the people with whom you enjoy it.

1. Smörgåstårta (sandwich cake)

Traditional buffet dish with countless varieties

The sandwich cake (smörgåstårta) is a particularly Swedish phenomenon that was formerly a must-have at large celebration. Sandwich cakes are both simple to make ahead of time and a great way to amaze visitors with lush layers and elegant embellishments. A Swedish sandwich cake is more than simply bread piled with creamy contents like shellfish or cold cuts - it's a work of art covered with vegetables and eggs, rolls of cheese, smoked meats or roast beef, artfully positioned dill sprigs, and a rainbow of colors. Try one of the charming tiny cafés in Stockholm's fairy tale neighborhood of Gamla Stan for some sandwich cake.

2. Palt (Swedish potato dumpling)

Every culture, it is said, has its dumplings, and Sweden is no exception. This delicious northern specialty is comprised largely of pork and potato. Raw potatoes are mashed or shredded and combined with flour to form dough, which is then formed into a ball around a succulent pork filling. After that, it's cooked in salt water and eaten with butter and lingo berry jam.

Restaurant Knut on Upplandsgatan in Stockholm is a fantastic spot to try these delectable dumplings since it is famed for its food from the northern area of Norrland, where this dumpling originated.

3. Pyttipanna (Swedish hash)

A conventional mash-up that has become a restaurant staple

Pyttipanna is a hash-like meal that was created as a quick method to use up the week's leftovers. It's made out of diced potatoes, roughly chopped onion, and little fragments of meat from previous meals. If you have some bacon and meatballs on hand, they work fantastic together. Add a fried egg and some pickled beets and you've got yourself a whole supper! Originally a home-cooked concoction, pyttipanna is now a popular lunch choice in Swedish restaurants. While in Stockholm, stop by Kvarnen Restaurant on the island of Södermalm to try this Swedish cooking staple.

4. Pork-Flavored Baked Beans

Lunchtime sweet and sour classic

Many of the cuisines often associated with Sweden may be found throughout the country, but brown beans are so Swedish that the EU protects their designation of origin. To utilize the protected title, the beans must be cultivated on the island of Land. The basic recipe is made by boiling the beans in water, then combining them with potato flour and adding a dash of vinegar and syrup for that familiar sweet and sour flavor. Traditionally, the beans are served with fried slices of salty bacon; however, some argue that they should be served with boiled potatoes.

5. Burger Patties Drenched With Onion Sauce

A worldwide classic with a Swedish twist

Swedish burger patties (pannbiff) are closely connected to a variety of similar meals from around Northern Europe, but this does not diminish their significance in the realm of classic Swedish cuisine. Beef or pork (or a combination of the two) is combined with breadcrumbs and milk to produce a tiny and compact patty in Sweden. The traditional onion sauce, produced by adding friend onion and cream to a standard roux, is an important addition. Panbiff is a simple meal that is popular in Swedish homes across the country on weekdays. It's also on the menu at numerous eateries around lunchtime. Don't forget about the lingonberry jam!

6. Kålpudding (cabbage pudding)

Turkish ingenuity has become a Swedish institution.

Cabbage pudding (kålpudding) is a filling classic and a reduced form of the filled rolls introduced from Türkiye to Sweden during an exchange era in the late 17th century. The original rolls were prepared of vine leaves, which ingenious Swedes replaced with cabbage. Traditional cabbage puddings are made with white cabbage, minced beef, and rice and are typically served with boiled potatoes, lingonberry jam, and either gravy or clarified butter.

Book a seat at Hasselbacken Restaurant in Djurgården to experience this classic meal for yourself.

7. Pancakes with Pea Soup

A Thursday custom in Swedish homes

Thursdays are typically served with pea soup and pancakes. According to legend, this was done because the country's once-Catholic populace required a big lunch before Friday's fast. Swedes have been eating this traditional soup since the 13th century, albeit the inclusion of pancakes came later. Yellow peas, pig broth, onions, and spices including thyme, marjoram, and mustard are common ingredients in the meal. You may get it in cans and cartons at your local grocery store, or look for it on daily lunch menus across town, especially on Thursdays.

8. Herring Fried

Swedish cuisine's most significant seafood

When we think of Swedish food, the first thing that springs to mind is generally herring, and it's a prominent component during Christmas, Easter, and Midsummer festivals. Herring, which is sometimes served pickled and sometimes served fresh, is popular seafood among Swedes. Traditionally, it is cooked in butter before being thrown in flour to achieve a delightfully crunchy top. It's frequently served with boiling potatoes or potato mash, and occasionally with a dab of lingo berry jam. Fried herring is an easy meal to make and a popular street food item in Stockholm.

9. Falukorv (falu sausage)

Super easy, but super yummy

Falu sausage (falukorv) is so Swedish that the term has been trademarked, first in Sweden and then throughout the EU. There are several ways to serve this enormous horseshoe sausage, but the original method is to pack and cook it in the oven. Incisions in the sausage are made and packed with onion, tomato, mustard, and cheese. The entire thing is then cooked and served with potato mash. It couldn't be simpler, but don't be fooled: this classic Swedish sausage is rich with flavor and makes the ideal, comforting meal on a chilly northern night.

10. Kalops (Swedish beef stew)

A Swedish version of boeuf bourguignon

Kalops is a traditional Swedish cuisine that consists of a thick stew of slow-cooked beef seasoned with onions, black pepper, and bay leaf. With a few carrots, the meal will quickly resemble a traditional French boeuf bourguignon, but the truth is that kalops is even older than its renowned French relative. Kalops with boiled potatoes and pickled beetroots is a popular lunch choice in Stockholm eateries. But the recipe is very simple to prepare and takes a long time to simmer on the stove, making it ideal for cooking in company while sipping a bottle of wine.

11. Lingonberry

These lovely red berries appear on practically every table in Stockholm. The popular fruit has the flavor and appearance of a cranberry and grows throughout Scandinavia. Swedish people enjoy lingonberries in jam, which they pair with meatballs, steak, potatoes, and porridge.

12. Meatballs

The Swedish meatball, or kjøttboller, may be found at congested IKEA snack shops, school lunch plates, and restaurants of all levels. Over decades, the meatball spread around the globe, establishing a comfortable popularity across Europe, but it acquired a specific position in Nordic countries. In Sweden, meatballs float in pools of brown gravy alongside complimentary sides like mashed potatoes, pickles, and lingonberries.

13. Crayfish

The sound of breaking crustacean shells fills the summer air in Stockholm. For Swedes, warm weather means crayfish parties full of fun and shellfish. Wear fancy paper hats and plastic bibs while devouring the salty summer delicacy's icy white flesh. The lean meat not only provides a nutritious supper, but it also serves as the glue that holds family and friends together throughout the hot summer months.

The Top 9 Fika Cafés in Stockholm

Make your coffee break or 'fika' in Stockholm an adventure in and of itself by exploring the city's vast array of cafés, coffee bars, patisseries, and bistros. Many bright and modern cafés in central Stockholm prioritize exceptional service and offer both energizing meals and a comfortable area to meet with everyone from close friends to business connections.

There are also several lovely patisseries with distinctive and green outdoor dining spaces where you may linger over a cup of steaming coffee. A stop in the capital frequently transports you back to the 1800s, the 1950s, or to timelessly charming European countries such as Italy or France. Explore the world, learn about history, and get to know Stockholm one taste at a time.

1. Sturekatten

Nostalgic Sturekatten is the place to go for a simple yet good lunch and some excellent, traditional pastries in a lovely setting that feels like a turn-of-the-century historical house. Sturekatten serves salads, open sandwiches, soups, and basic lunch meals like quiche Lorraine, but it's their sweet pastries created from old housewife recipes from the 1930s that bring the most customers. Chocolate butter cream macaroons and hazelnut meringue roulades are two lesser-known Swedish staples. This lovely and ancient café, one of Stockholm's oldest, is located on Riddaregatan, about 50 meters from the Östermalmstorg Metro Station. If you'd rather take a stroll to whet your appetite, it's only a 15-minute walk from Stockholm Central Station.

- The address is Riddargatan 4, 114 35 Stockholm, Sweden.
- **Operating hours**: 9 a.m. to 7 p.m., Monday through Friday., Saturday, 9 am to 6 pm, and Sunday, 10 a
- **Phone**: +46 8 6111612

2. Helin, Flickorna

Flickorna Helin serves traditional Swedish pastries and skillfully designed seasonal cuisine on a magnificent patio by the Djurgrden Well Canal (Djurgrdsbrunnskanalen) or by their open fireplace. Classic buns and Swedish jam biscuits, as well as rich and inventive cheesecakes, exquisite French macaroons, and much more, are all on their delectable menu, along with energizing smoothies, fresh salads, and hearty main courses. On the island of Djurgrden, Flickorna Helin is housed in the fascinating and inspirational Scanian Mine (Sknska Gruvan) structure. Its position makes it ideal for relaxing your feet after a busy day at the Skansen open-air museum or visiting the adjacent Vasa Museum or ABBA Museum. Nordiska Museet/Vasamuseet, the nearest tram station, is only 500 meters away.

- The address is Rosendalsvägen 14, 115 21 Stockholm, Sweden.
- **Hours of operation**: Monday-Saturday 9 a.m.-5 p.m., Sunday 10 a.m.-5 p.m.
- **Phone**: +46 8 6645108

3. Saturnus Café

Café Saturnus is ideal for anybody looking for an elegant, continental experience or who is ready for the task of sampling the café's famous large cinnamon bun. When you arrive at Café Saturnus, their maître d' will lead you to your seat and encourage you to taste one of their many delicious pastries or a typical café meal consisting of an open sandwich, salad, or an omelet with a French twist. Café Saturnus is located just over 50 meters from the

Eriksbergsgatan Bus Stop in Stockholm's lush Humlegrden Park on the island of Östermalm.

The nearest metro station is located on Rdmansgatan, about a 5-minute walk from the café.

- **Address**: Eriksbergsgatan 6, 114 30 Stockholm, Sweden
- **Hours of operation**: Monday-Friday 8 a.m.-6 p.m., Saturday-Sunday 9 a.m.-6 p.m.
- **Phone**: +46 8 6117700

4. Trädgrdscafé Rosendals

Inside a quaint greenhouse environment, Rosendals Trädgrdscafé serves certified organic items as well as seasonal open sandwiches and pastries. In the summer, you may have your coffee outside in the apple grove, and in the winter, you can warm up by the fire inside the greenhouse. The lunch buffet features biodynamic vegetables, fruits, and herbs grown in the garden. All breads and pastries are baked in their wood-fired oven. Rosendals Trädgrdscafé is located in the magnificent Rosendal Garden (Rosendals Trädgrd) on the island of Djurgården. So combine your coffee break with a stroll through the lovely gardens. Parking is available immediately next to the café, or you can take the tram to Bellmansro, which is around 400 meters away.

- The address is Rosendalsterrassen 12, 115 21 Stockholm, Sweden.
- **Phone**: +46 8 54581270

5. Petissan Kafé

Kafé Petissan is set in a charming small wooden structure with turn-of-the-century furniture, and they've been selling coffee here since 1870, despite significant changes over the years. It was originally called the Petit Café, but the name was swiftly Swedish into the more manageable Petissan. go inside and go back in time with a hot cup of coffee in one hand and a classic Swedish bun or biscuit in the other, or indulge in a slice of seasonal cake or pie after a busy day of adventure on Djurgården's amusement island. Kafé Petissan is housed within Skansen, an exquisite open-air museum on the island of Djurgrden. Skansen and Liljevalchs/Gröna Lund are the closest tram stops.

- Address: Djurgårdsslätten 49, 115 21, Stockholm, Sweden
- Open daily from 11 a.m. to 4 p.m.
- Phone: +46 8 6634778

6. Vetekatten

Vetekatten is one of Stockholm's oldest patisseries and has become something of a Stockholm institution, famous for its classic biscuits, cosmopolitan pastries, creative pralines, and spectacular cakes. Classic lunch foods such as salads, soups, and open sandwiches may be enjoyed in this timeless atmosphere, which bears tribute to Sweden's rich history of coffee. Vetekatten has locations around Stockholm, but their most iconic patisserie, going back to the 1920s, is located on Kungsgatan, just steps away from Stockholm Central Station. If you prefer to travel by metro, there is a direct entry from the T-Central Metro Station.

- Address: 55 Kungsgatan, 111 22 Stockholm, Sweden

- Hours of operation: Monday-Friday 7:30 a.m.-8 p.m., Saturday-Sunday 9:30 a.m.-8 p.m.
- Phone: +46 8 208405

7. Café Foam

Café Foam, a vibrant and modern coffee and pastry shop, is arguably most known for its outstanding American-style brunch menu. This restaurant is all about design and local, organic food. Visit on a Sunday afternoon for scrambled eggs and pancakes, or stay for lunch and sample their weekly salad, soup, or pasta dish. And don't forget to try their fair-trade coffee, which was created in collaboration with the Love Coffee micro-roaster in Lund, Sweden. Café Foam is located in the central area of Östermalm, just a short distance from Karlaplan Plaza. Skeppargatan and Nybrogatan are the nearest bus stops, both of which are less than 100 meters from the café.

- **Address**: Stockholm, Sweden Karlavägen 75, 114 49
- **Hours of operation**: Monday-Friday 8 a.m.-6 p.m., Saturday-Sunday 9 a.m.-5 p.m.
- **Phone**: +46 8 6600996

8. Ritorno

Ritorno is worth a visit not just for its delectable and classic baked products like carrot cake, apple mazarin cake, almond and cardamon buns, fresh bread rolls, and rye bread, but also for the beautiful vintage feel inside. The proprietors have chosen to keep the vintage 50s and 60s vibe from the early days of contemporary café culture. Ritorno has various sites across Stockholm, but its original location is on Odengatan, in the center of Vasastaden. This lovely old building, complete with crystal chandeliers in the ceiling and oil paintings on the walls, is just next to the Dalagatan Bus Stop and a 5-minute walk from the S: t Eriksplan Metro Station.

- **Address**: 80 Odengatan, 113 22 Stockholm, Sweden
- **Operating hours**: 7 am to 10 pm, Monday through Thursday. Friday, 7 a.m. to 8 p.m., Saturday, 8 am to 6 pm, and Sunday,
- **Phone**: +46 8 320106

9. France Petite

Petite France is the ideal patisserie whether you're in the mood for a classic mille-feuille, éclair, macaron, croissant, pain au chocolat, or crème brûlée - simply put, their whole menu is an ode to classic French baking. Come in for a decadent goat's cheese salad, confit duck, or a slice of quiche Lorraine for lunch. On weekends, they also provide a traditional French breakfast. Petite France is in Stockholm's Kungsholmen area. The John Ericssonsgatan Bus Stop is just next door. If you prefer to take the metro, get off at Fridhemsplan or Rdhuset, both of which are about a 10-minute walk from the café.

- **Address**: 6 John Ericssonsgatan, 112 22 Stockholm, Sweden
- Monday: 7 a.m. to 6 p.m., Tuesday-Friday: 7 a.m. to 7 p.m., Saturday-Sunday: 7 a.m. to 5 p.
- **Phone**: +46 8 6182800

EXERCISE

Where Did You Intend To Eat?

_____
_____
_____
_____
_____

Which Of The Meal Are You Trying Or Did You Have Another Plan For What To Eat?

_____
_____
_____
_____
_____
_____
_____
_____
_____
_____
_____

What Are Your Experience With The Food And Fika Cafes You Visited?

_____
_____
_____
_____
_____
_____
_____
_____
_____
_____
_____
_____
_____
_____
_____
_____
_____

CHAPTER FOUR

Stockholm Transportation Guide

Here's how to use Stockholm's public transportation like a native, whether by bus, tram, commuter train, or boat. When it comes to public transit, Stockholm is a visitor's dream. The city's subway system is simple and efficient, and it operates late at night on weekends. Buses, trams, commuter trains, and ferries connect the capital's 14 islands, as well as all of its key attractions. Almost all of these choices are run by the same business, Storstockholms Lokaltrafik (SL), making it simple to transition between means of transportation.

For a 75-minute ride, paper or mobile tickets cost 44 SEK. However, if you anticipate making numerous travels, it's typically better value to get a plastic SL card for 20 SEK and load it with credit, or to purchase a 24-hour, 72-hour, or weekly ticket. Whether you're looking for your accommodation or simply want to get lost in the city and then locate a wonderful bar or restaurant along the road.

Stockholm's Public Transportation Options

Subway

The tunnelbana, Stockholm's large subterranean network, is made up of three color-coded lines (green, red, and blue) that divide into distinct branches on the outskirts of the capital. Subway trains normally operate between 5 a.m. and 1 a.m. throughout the week, with late-night service on Fridays and Saturdays—very convenient in a city where cabs are pricey. At ground level, stations in the city center are often well-marked with huge 'T' signs. Every station has wheelchair and stroller access, albeit not necessarily at every exit. Tickets must be purchased in advance at subway stations, Pressbyrn, and 7-11 convenience stores.

Bus

The bus network in Stockholm is more difficult to handle than the subway, and it's not worth it if you're only coming for a short time or plan to do most of your traveling during the day. Buses, on the other hand, are a terrific alternative if you need to go after 1 a.m. during the week when the subway is closed. Services are well-heated and generally pleasant and secure. Line 4 (which becomes Nightbus 94) between Radiohuset and Gullmarsplan is the main inner-city night route. On all buses, SL cards are accepted. If you don't have a ticket, you may pay using the SL app; a 75-minute travel costs 44 SEK (compared to 31 SEK with an SL card).

Train

With a single SL ticket, you can travel surprisingly far outside the city limits, making Stockholm's aboveground rail network a popular choice for both commuters and weekend day-trippers. The harbors of Nynästamn and Saltsjöbaden are both famous tourist destinations. Sigtuna, Sweden's oldest town, may also be accessed by taking an SL train to Märsta and then a short bus journey. If you're traveling from Stockholm to Uppsala, you'll need to purchase a separate UL ticket, or if you've previously purchased an all-inclusive SL ticket for 24 hours or more, you may purchase an SL ticket extension.

The latter is best arranged through an SL counter; ticket machines are available but might be confusing for first-time guests.

Tram

Trams service Djurgården Island, which is home to several of Stockholm's most prominent museums. The Line 7 service is available from two nearby stops in the city center: Hamngatan and Nybrokajan. Both stops are within walking distance of the central station, as well as the metro stations Östermalmstorg and Kungsträdgrden. Tram line 22 serves the city's outskirts. Valid SL cards or mobile tickets must be purchased in advance and displayed on board at subway stations or convenience stores.

Ferry

In Stockholm, using the ferry seldom saves time, but it is a pleasant and picturesque way to get about, especially during excellent weather. The Djurgården boat links Slussen (follow indications from the Södermalmstorg metro exit) to Djurgrden Island, stopping often at Skeppsholmen (check with staff before boarding). The Sjövägen 80 boat line runs between downtown Nybroplan (near the Kungsträdgrden metro stop) and Frihamnen port, stopping at Djurgården Island along the route. SL tickets are valid for both services but must be purchased ahead of time. Several commercial firms also operate boats from the city center to the Stockholm archipelago. The two largest are Waxholmsbolaget and Stromma.

Road Trips Around Stockholm

Away from the city's renowned attractions, you'll find a treasure trove of hidden, gorgeous, and historical environs - so make the time to explore these intriguing sites within 1 hour of Stockholm. Viking remnants, medieval castle ruins, majestic Renaissance palaces, both modern and classic art, charming villages, award-winning retail complexes, old woodlands in brilliant greens, and healthy archipelago experiences may all be found just outside the city. Whether you're driving or taking use of the region's well-developed public transportation system, there are plenty of places to visit near Stockholm for both kids and adults.

1. Birka

Birka is a world heritage site with an intriguing Viking village and instructive installations for people of all ages. The island's beautiful position on Lake Mälaren made it an ideal trade outpost over a thousand years ago, but it doesn't assist in getting there now. Fortunately, public boats service the island well. Stroll throughout Viking settlements, listen to an experienced guide, and let the youngsters try their hand at practical crafts like candlemaking or jewelry making. There are lots of excellent places to stop for food or a swim, so why not make it a day trip?

2. Uppsala

Uppsala is a lovely and bustling town with a rich history and a slower pace of life than its larger neighbor. The city is only 43 miles north of Stockholm and can be reached in less than 40 minutes by high-speed train. Once you've arrived, join a guided tour for professional insights from a local guide, or go it alone and get lost along the quiet river or amid the city's lovely streets. Make a point of seeing the magnificent church. If you want to walk through old surroundings, go to the Gamla Uppsala archeological site and museum. Uppsala is also a fantastic spot to go shopping or relax with a coffee and a cinnamon bun. Before you go, pick up a souvenir from the city's hip artisan cooperative Öster om Ån.

3. Sigtuna

Before Stockholm, there existed Sigtuna, presently a charming tiny town that is proud of its historical significance. Sigtuna is an excellent day-trip destination because of its convenient location about 30 miles north of Stockholm. Discover some of the more than 150 rune stones in Sigtuna. Visit the Sigtuna Museum to discover more about life in Sweden's historic political center, as well as the location of the first Swedish coinage. If you're interested in technology and aviation, go to Arlanda Flygsamlingar, which is just outside of town and has propeller planes and a flying simulator.

4. Runriket (Rune Kingdom)

Rune Kingdom (Runriket) is home to several remarkably well-preserved Viking-era rune stones. This historically significant location is about 24 miles north of Stockholm, surrounding Vallentuna Lake. Check out the beautiful rune snakes in Fällbro and Gällsta, carved by the very active runemaster, Öpnir. Before having a picnic by the lake, stop at the Arkils Assembly (Arkils tingstad), which is marked by stones. If you time your visit to coincide with Rune Kingdom Day, you will be able to eat some traditional Viking meals as well as see the Vikings manufacture handicrafts, and engage in warfare.

5. National Park of Tyresta

Tyresta National Park is magnificent, old woodland about 18 miles south of Stockholm. The most convenient method to get there from the capital is by vehicle, although a mix of metros and buses will also bring you there in approximately an hour. Begin your visit to Naturum, where you can learn more about Sweden's national parks and obtain information about trails and guided excursions. Then embark on your trip through the lush forest, following one of the defined routes that range in length from 1.5 to 8.5 kilometers.

- **Address**: Svartbäckens by 361, 136 59 Vendelsö, Sweden.
- **Phone**: +46 8 745 33 94

6. Södertälje

The lovely town of Södertälje is filled with picture-perfect architecture, regal buildings, and fantastic lakeside attractions. The town is only 24 miles southwest of Stockholm and is easily accessible by public transportation. Spend a bright day outside Tullgarn Palace, the summer residence of Swedish King Gustaf V. Explore the Södertälje Art Gallery, which hosts fun programs for youngsters at regular intervals. Alternatively, enjoy an unforgettable excursion out onto Lake Mälaren onboard a true steamer from the past. Don't forget to visit the picturesque open-air museum of Torekällberget, where you may interact with the animals and purchase a gift to take home.

7. Kurva Kungens

Kungens Kurva is a sprawling business district filled with popular stores selling everything from fashion and jewelry to home décor and sporting equipment. Kungens Kurva is only 6 miles from central Stockholm, and while driving is the most convenient method to get there, the region is also well served by local transportation from Hornstull. Sporting clothing and equipment may be found in the Swedish brand Stadium or the French retailer Decathlon, as well as Swedish fashion at H&M and the newest

American styles at Lexington, with lots of food alternatives for lunch.

8. Enköping

Enköping is a pretty small town with numerous old buildings and idyllic open areas. The village is 43 miles north of Stockholm and can be reached by rail in less than 40 minutes, making it ideal for a stress-free day trip from the large metropolis. Stroll through floral and green parks like the more than a century-old Afzeliiplan, the beautiful Drömparken (lit. Dream Park), or the diminutive small English Park (Engelska parken). If you enjoy history, you should visit the medieval castles and remains of Husby Holme, Borgarringen, and Gröneborg. If you like your castles to remain majestic and preserved, visit neighboring Fiholm Castle or ngsö Castle.

9. Mariefred

Visiting Mariefred is like traveling back in time to a fairy tale village complete with cobblestone streets, gorgeous castles, and traditional traditions. Mariefred is located on the beaches of Lake Mälaren, approximately 45 miles west of Stockholm. The quickest method to get here is by automobile, but if you don't want to drive, a mix of trains and buses will bring you here in approximately an hour from the center of Stockholm. Visit the stately, red Gripsholm Castle, which is not only an amazing structure in a stunning setting but also houses the Swedish state's portrait collection. While in the neighborhood, take advantage of the opportunity to go by riverboat or enjoy some modern art at the neighboring POM Gallery.

10. Nynäshamn

Nynäshamn is the archipelago's gem, overflowing with stunning environments and historical monuments. The island is approximately 37 miles from central Stockholm. You may arrive by vehicle or by commuter rail. Visit the Nynäshamn Visitor Centre for further information on where to discover the various artworks. Enjoy the vistas of the archipelago by traversing the Baltic Sea or the Draget Canal, and then remain for a moment to observe Sweden's oldest lighthouse. Stop at Tostesta Felag and explore the Iron Age residence for some living history that will enchant the entire family.

EXERCISE

What Are Your Experience With The Transportation System In Stockholm And How Did You Navigate The Road Trip?

_____
_____
_____
_____
_____
_____
_____
_____
_____
_____
_____
_____
_____
_____
_____
_____
_____
_____

CHAPTER FIVE

Stockholm's Best Islands

What could be better than venturing out and discovering some of Stockholm's greatest islands? Stockholm's archipelago is bursting with magnificent scenery, a friendly atmosphere, and delicious food. varied islands provide varied experiences; some conceal real archipelago towns far apart from the hustle and bustle of the main metropolis, surrounded by gorgeous forests and fishing seas, while others feature a diverse array of restaurants, vibrant nightclubs, and small taverns. If you don't want to leave the city, you may take a boat out for a half-day excursion in the sun. Or perhaps you'd rather spend a whole weekend away from the mainland, surrounded by ancient history and beautiful nature?

1. Vaxholm

Vaxholm is sometimes referred to as the capital of the Stockholm Archipelago, which seems an appropriate title given everything the little town has to offer. The lovely small-town atmosphere, as well as the numerous historic buildings, charming streets, intriguing cafés, and hospitable restaurants, draw a large number of visitors each year. Vaxholm Fortress (Vaxholms Fästning) is situated on the island, where you may learn about the area's history. Vaxholm's proximity to the center of Stockholm makes it an ideal site to visit if you're short on time. The village is around 40 minutes by vehicle from the center of Stockholm. Alternatively, a more adventurous method to get to the island is to take a boat at Strömkajen Ferry Terminal, where you can expect a one-hour voyage.

2. Sandhamn

Despite its slightly greater distance from Stockholm, Sandhamn is a popular archipelago destination with lots to see and do, as well as a busy nightlife. The island is located on the archipelago's rim and may be reached by boat in a few hours from the city. When you arrive, you'll discover a lovely island town complete with quaint stores, restaurants, and cafés, as well as some wonderful beaches, good swimming rocks, and gorgeous pine trees. Hike one of the hiking paths, have a picnic on the sun-kissed rocks, or simply relax on one of the island's many gorgeous sandy beaches. Sandholm is frequently connected with vitality, movement, and celebrations. In a nightclub, you may dance the night away or enjoy a drink in a nice piano bar.

3. Möja

Peaceful Möja is an excellent site to enjoy a real archipelago experience, complete with stunning scenery and a slower pace of life on a vibrant island. Möja is one of the bigger islands, with hundreds of permanent residents, a school, a post office, stores, numerous restaurants, a church, a local history museum, guest ports, and several types of lodging. The island is the ideal location to unwind, with paddling, hiking, and cycling taking precedence over late evenings in crowded taverns. The woodlands are also abundant in berries, and many people come to enjoy the excellent fishing sites on the island. Because Möja is located on the outskirts of the archipelago's center, the boat ride from Stockholm takes around 3 hours.

4. Utö

The popular island of Utö attracts many people due to its beautiful beaches, tasty food, and fantastic lodgings with breathtaking views. The mining and military history of the island may also be learned at the Mining and Local History Museum (Gruv- och Hembygdsmuseet). Climb to the top of the windmill for a magnificent view of the island and the sea. Utö is also an excellent island for cycling. You can go from north to south in roughly an hour. Stop for a bite to eat in Gruvbyn (lit. Mine Town) before finishing the day with a swim at one of the islands sandy beaches in the south. Utö may be reached in less than three hours from central Stockholm.

5. Finnhamn

Finnhamn is an archipelago staple, and any vacation here will undoubtedly result in spectacular nature, a refreshing plunge, and delicious food. Craggy rocks, pine trees, and oak groves wait, with lots of opportunities for a saltwater swim, beautiful hiking paths, and fascinating cycling routes. Many visitors to the island opt to rent a canoe and experience the island's gorgeous landscape from the water. Finnhamn also has an organic farm shop where you may buy organic vegetables and handcrafted treats to enjoy on weekends.

Because Finnhamn is located on the outskirts of the archipelago, the boat ride from central Stockholm will take around 2 1/2 hours.

6. Grinda

Grinda's distinctive beauty and proximity to downtown Stockholm (only an hour by boat) make it one of the archipelago's most popular islands. The entire island is a nature reserve, with agriculture, animal husbandry, rocky outcrops, and both deciduous and pine woods for pleasant hikes. The island is ideal for families with children since there are several animals to see, including chickens, cows, and sheep, as well as numerous swimming locations, both from the beach and from cliffs. Grinda also provides possibilities to admire unique architecture. Check out Grinda Guest House (Grinda Wärdshus), which is one of the archipelagos largest and most magnificent stone mansions in art nouveau style.

7. Kymmendö

Kymmendö can offer diversified nature, rural appeal, and small-scale feelings away from the city's stress and bustle. The island is a true archipelago island in every respect, with grazing horses and sheep, several wet meadows and exquisite flowery meadows, as well as some lovely hazel and oak slopes. The island's only combination shop and restaurant is only open in the summer, so if you visit during the off-season, bring a picnic basket and have your lunch on the island. In the spring, summer, and fall, you may take the Vaxholm Ferry from Dalarö to Kymmendö. The only way to get here in the winter is via a taxi boat if the water hasn't frozen over!

8. Fjäderholmarna

Fjäderholmarna is the cities nearest Archipelago Island, and it's a terrific area to enjoy stunning surroundings, peaceful swimming places, and great cafés. This island, which is only 20 minutes distant from Nybrokajen, is ideal for an archipelago day excursion. Throughout the island, you'll find calm rocks where you can sunbathe and swim, and if you're hungry or thirsty, you'll have no trouble finding exactly what you're looking for, whether it's a full dinner or simply a gelato. Fjäderholmarna also has its chocolate factory where you may try some handcrafted pralines. The island also has a variety of artisan shops and workshops that sell items produced from wool, glass, and clay.

9. Svartsö

Svartsö is a reasonably large pastoral island with hotels, restaurants, stores, and a school. Lace-up your sneakers for a trek or run around the island, or hire a bicycle and fly by meadows, lakes, and pastures dotted with grazing animals. If you visit during the winter, put on a pair of cross-country skis for a truly unique exploring experience. Culture vultures will appreciate Svartsö's abundance of concerts, talks, and exhibitions, as well as its annual summer culture week. Svartsö is a small island in the Stockholm Archipelago. The boat ride from the center of Stockholm takes around 2 1/2 hours.

10. Arholma

Arholma is one of the larger and more well-known islands in the Stockholm Archipelago, featuring authentic architecture, various intriguing attractions, and some excellent biking and walking paths, not to mention rugged cliffs and sandy beaches for swimming. Coastal cannons and rock shelters harken back to a time when the island was utilized for defense and are likely to pique the interest of history aficionados. If you're looking for more thrills, try the island's zip line or whoosh through the jungle on mountain bike paths. Arholma is located in the northern part of the Stockholm Archipelago and is accessible by boat from Simpnäs regularly. The trip takes about 15 minutes. During the spring and summer months, boats also depart from central Stockholm and Norrtälje.

Stockholm's Best Hotels

1. Scandic's Downtown Camper

Scandic's Downtown Camper is ideal for people who lead an active lifestyle. Not only is it conveniently positioned near all of the major attractions, including the waterfront and Stockholm Central Station, but the hotel also offers everyday activities for visitors, such as running, walks, workshops, cinema evenings, and DJs. There's also a gym, pool, spa, and yoga lessons on-site. In addition, the foyer has a range of skateboards, kayaks, and bikes for rent. There are several excellent dining options around the hotel, but it also boasts a grill restaurant that provides delicious comfort cuisine.

- What's close by? A short eight-minute walk to Stockholm Central Station, as well as several stores, parks, and restaurants.
- **Price range**: Not bad for a couple of nights in Stockholm's core.
- **Time Out tip**: On a tight budget? The activities at Downtown Camper are free for guests, making it a cost-effective option. If you're traveling with a group, there's no need to text across the corridor; simply arrange linked rooms.

2. The Bank Hotel

Bank Hotel is a premium hotel in the center of Stockholm, housed in a historic bank building (as the name suggests). The interiors, on the other hand, are everything but bank-like, with soft furnishings, contemporary fixtures, and a mood that is anything from Wall Street. Flat-screen TVs, minibars, coffee machines, and complimentary toiletries and slippers are among the luxurious facilities. On-site, there's a casual eating restaurant with a high-end vibe and Le Hibou, a cocktail terrace bar with amazing views of the city from the top level. Darling, chin-chin.

- **What's close by?** It's rather central, having both Strandvagen for high-end shopping and Stureplan for nightlife within walking distance.
- **Price range**: A reasonably priced weekend getaway that becomes much more affordable when shared with a roommate.
- **Time Out suggestion**: Fancy a slow breakfast with bubbles? The only remedy is to raise a glass and bite into eggs Benedict the way the good Brunch-Lord intended at Bonnie's on-site restaurant. You will have the option of a buffet or an al la carte meal accompanied by champagne.

3. The Lydmar Hotel

Stay at the historic archive building of the Swedish National Museum to soak up some local history. Built in 1829, this lovely establishment was refurbished in 2008 by the Small Luxury Hotel Group. Each room is uniquely furnished, with sleek, contemporary furnishings and artwork on the walls.

This motif is carried throughout the hotel, with artwork ranging from 1900 to the current day on display. Room amenities include a minibar, TV, and air conditioning.

- **What's close by?** Nearby attractions include Stureplan Square, the seaside, and the freshly rebuilt National Museum.
- **Price range**: Expensive, but worth it for the tranquil waterfront views and the melt-in-your-mouth steak tartare (sorry, vegetables).
- **Time Out tip**: Like most tourists, you'll want to see as many sights as possible, but how can you do it efficiently? Get a Go City All-Inclusive Pass (just under £60) to gain admission to over 50 activities across the city, including sightseeing cruises.

4. Hotel Nordic Light

This modern hotel, located around 100 meters from Stockholm Central Station, epitomizes sleek Nordic flair. Floods of light will pour in via large windows, and original artworks will be exhibited in the foyer as part of the 'artist in residence' program. The rooms also have rainfall showers, premium beds designed by Swedish designer Hilding Anders, complimentary amenities, a TV, and a safe large enough to fit a laptop. Lykke, the hotel's in-house restaurant, provides modern Nordic cuisine and serves an organic breakfast that includes everything from fresh fruit to sweet, fluffy American pancakes.

- **What's close by?** The hotel is ideally located near the Arlanda Airport Express Train, Sergals Torg, and Drottinggatan, Stockholm's lively retail center.

- **Price range**: An inexpensive and bright minimalist fantasy realized.
- **Time Out tip**: Visit the dazzling department store Nordiska Kompaniet, where you'll find anything from jewelry to pottery, whether you're seeking a traditional souvenir for your travels or just want a little window shopping.

5. Berns Hotel

This is the Stockholm hotel where Edith Piaf once sang, Marlene Dietrich had her dressing room, and Axl Rose once bit a security officer on the leg (dropping his Converse high-tops in the process, which the hotel gave away 10 years later on Instagram). Hotel Berns is more than simply a place to sleep at night; it also houses an internationally famous musical theater, where everyone from the Supremes to Rihanna has performed.

- **What's close by?** Right close to Nybrokajen Harbour, with panoramic views of Berzelii Park and Stockholm Palace. Of course, Stureplan is available for a night in the town.
- **Price range**: Look for fairly priced and comfortable accommodations for a three-night stay.
- **Time Out tip**: Book a table at Terransen at Berns while the night is still young to enjoy colorful drinks and views of Nybriviken Bay and Berzelli Park.

6. Hotel Rival

Hotel Rival, owned by former ABBA member Benny Andersson, is replete with subtle nods to the world-famous

Swedish pop group. Every one of the 99 rooms has a cutting-edge entertainment system, a 32-inch plasma screen, and access to a collection of DVDs and music from - whom else? - ABBA. The property has an old-school cabaret ambiance thanks to plush red velvet sofas, cinematic and theatrical elements, and elegant lighting.

- What's close by? Mariatorget Square is right next door, and Old Town is about a 10-minute walk away.
- **Price range**: Moderately priced beautiful art deco rooms with plenty of space and picturesque views.
- **Time Out tip**: Why not conclude the year in a unique way in Stockholm? Rivals Watson Bar hosts a lavish New Year's Eve event, complete with an exquisite seafood plate matched with delectable French wines.

7. Hotel the Winery

Guests are invited to follow the winemaking process from barrel to bottle at the Winery Hotel. Enjoy a relaxing sampling at the bar or panoramic views from the heated pool on the upper patio. The 184 guest rooms all have an industrial vibe to them, with exposed brick walls, high ceilings and windows, and brass embellishments. Daily activities organized by the hotel's skilled sommeliers may include learning how to open a champagne bottle with a saber or indulging in a Kundalini yoga and wine session.

- What's close by? Friends Arena and the Mall of Scandinavia are nearby. Furthermore, public transportation may get you to Central Station in less than 30 minutes.

- **Price range**: A low-cost stay somewhere absolutely distinctive, great for wine enthusiasts or special events.
- **Time Out tip:** Gallo Nero on-site has it all when it comes to creating an ambient setting ideal for dining with friends or family. Local wine, supper, and dance are all available under one roof.

8. Hotel Skeppsholmen

Skeppsholmen was a hospital, a brief jail, and the royal naval barracks for the Swedish king's officers before becoming the island's lone hotel. Despite their more than 300-year age – and the fact that structural alterations are not permitted during restorations – the 81 guest rooms remain in good condition. Each room has sleek, modern furnishings, rustic décor, and plaques that educate you about the history of the area (and what happened in your room).

- What's close by? The hotel is remote yet well-connected, so you can simply take a boat to Old Town or a bus into town from Kastellholmsbron.
- **Price range**: Reasonably priced basic accommodations with great sea views.
- **Time Out tip**: How about a quickie tournament before lunch? Take out your tennis racket and walk down to the tennis court, which is right on the sea, so you can take in the sights.

9. Birger Jarl's

This little central hideaway provides excellent value in one of the world's most costly cities. Accommodation choices among the 271 guest rooms include freshly updated suites, junior suites, and studios. While the location puts you close to shopping, restaurants, and other attractions, you won't want to miss the 'after work' jazz evenings performed every Wednesday in the lobby bar.

- **What's close by?** Stureplan is a 10-minute walk away, and the ABBA Museum is within a stone's throw away.
- **Price range**: Enjoy a variety of inexpensive cozy, modern rooms with superb facilities while staying in a central location. Perf.
- **Time Out tip**: Include the breakfast that visitors can't quit talking about with your stay. From cold cuts to hot foods to seasonal fruits and pastries, we have it all. Yum.

10. Hotel Pop House

The Pop Hotel's common entrance with the Abba Museum, as well as the fact that one of its owners is former band member Björn Ulvaeus, will appeal to music fans. The hotel's 49 rooms, which are vividly designed with purple and lime green accents, are beautifully lit by panoramic sliding windows. The hotel is located near Gröna Lund amusement park, the Swedish Music Hall of Fame, and Skansen, one of the world's oldest museums, and is only a five-minute tram ride from the city center.

- **What's close by?** Only a five-minute tram ride into central Stockholm, with the Skansen Open-Air Museum, the Vasa Museum, and other attractions nearby.

- **Price range**: The rooms here are reasonably priced but attractive.
- **Time Out tip**: The Junior Suite is worth the money for die-hard Abba fans who can afford it. It's a stunning homage to the erstwhile 1970s super group, filled with Abba Gold Album memorabilia.

11. Ett Hem

Ett Hem, which means 'at home' in Swedish, is an appropriate name. And if your idea of home is sneaking tastes of baked apple cake from the kitchen while speaking with the chef about what you'd like for dinner or curling up with a novel beneath a sheepskin blanket, you've come to the right spot. This red brick townhouse exudes low-key beauty from the foyer to the bedroom. Guests may borrow bicycles and raincoats, as well as freshly squeezed juice from the fridge, play records on the hotel's functional phonograph, tickle the ivories at the grand piano, or rest in the bright, sunny conservatory. The hotel also has services for handicapped visitors to enhance their comfort throughout their stay.

- What's close by? The Royal Swedish Opera and Old Town are also nearby.
- **Price range**: We'll save you the actual cost of this charming country-esque five-star gem.
- **Time Out Tip**: Need a five-minute break? Ett Hem's private garden is the ideal personal place for delving into a book.

Stockholm's Best Airbnbs

Look no further than Stockholm, Sweden's peaceful capital, for a trip that is nothing but chilled vibes and magnificent scenery, culture, and gastronomy. The ABBA museum alone is worth the trip. To get you started, this Swedish city boasts some fantastic restaurants and pubs. If you want to go sightseeing, the city and neighboring areas have some great natural scenery. The Stockholm archipelago is home to a plethora of natural areas that may be explored by boat. A journey away, on the other hand, necessitates a tranquil and cool location to stay and recuperate, and Airbnb provides a plethora of excellent options. From luxurious metropolitan flats to offbeat eco-friendly group accommodations. We've compiled a list of the best to assist you with your planning.

1. Älvsjö Modest House for the Entire Family

If you're searching for something unique, this recently built small house could be for you. With a downstairs bedroom and a loft space, this little property in a great location is ideal for a group of friends or a family of four. It's also extremely well connected to the city's main neighborhoods, with just a short stroll via a park. The opulent apartment overlooks a well-kept garden where you can unwind in the sun (when you're not dancing to the built-in speakers inside).

2. The Island Hideaway in the Municipality Of Österåker

Stockholm isn't called 'beauty on water' for nothing. At this massive island hideaway, soak in the natural wonders of the archipelago. This contemporary three-bed (sleeps six) is surrounded by woods, is within walking distance of two beaches, and has a hot tub. Isn't it cool?

- How many rooms are there? Five. Sleeps six people.
- In the mood for an island getaway?
- Are there any location advantages? Much. Greenery.
- What is the budget range? The facilities make the price worthwhile.

3. Gamla Stans Bohemian Four-Sleeper

With so many blankets and soft furniture on display, it's difficult to believe you won't feel comfortable in this unusual abode. It's a far cry from the Scandi chic we've all grown accustomed to, but that's not always a bad thing. Furthermore, it is located in the calm Gamla Stan, making touring and relaxing in the evenings a breeze.

- How many rooms are there? One. Sleeps four people.
- Mood? Eclectic to the max.
- Are there any location advantages? In the center of Old Town, in a 17th-century mansion. Isn't that epic?
- Price range? Very reasonable.

4. Gamla Stans Strategically Placed Penthouse

Yes, this is an opulent penthouse. The ambiance is art-infused Scandi chic, but you'll be hard-pressed to find a four-bedroom property in this position, at this price, and with these stunning views of Stockholm from its rooftop terrace.

- How many rooms are there? Four. Sleeps nine people.
- Mood? Extra special.
- Location advantages include city views from your rooftop balcony. Live your life as if you are the queen or king you truly are.
- Budget range? Boujie but not extravagant.

5. Ostermalm's Antique Three-Bed

Do you have a flush? You'll be looking for a room on the top level of this old bank. It's simply coasters (ring marks on such antique furniture wouldn't be welcome). There's also a convenient fireplace to sit in front of, as well as a wall of books to read while you're there.

- Three rooms, sleeping four people.
- How about the mood? Hygge personified.
- Are there any location advantages? Super convenient location with easy access to the rest of the city.
- What is the budget range? Every cent was well spent.

6. Trollbäcken's Studio with a View

Would you like to wake up, get a cup of coffee, stroll outdoors, and find yourself actually on a lake?

You can have it all at this adorable studio house in Stockholm's Trollbäcken, complete with a large terrace and a panoramic lake view. You may either drive 25 minutes to Stockholm City or ride one of the two bikes available for a modest charge. There's even a shower outdoors so you can wash while admiring the scenery, as well as a BBQ and a 43-inch TV with Netflix and Chromecast. That's so cozy.

- How many rooms are there? One, which sleeps two people.
- In the mood? Lakehouse studio.
- Are there any location advantages? You're practically out on the water. Immerse yourself in the festivities.
- What is the budget range? Very reasonable, but requires a minimum of six nights.

7. The Chic Sofo Attic Apartment

Do you want to be in the middle of Hipsterville? SoFo (the district south of Folkungagatan) is well-known for its fashionable stores, cafés, and pubs. This two-bedroom apartment in a lovely 1880s building is perfect for an enviably sophisticated stay. Beautiful wood paneling, modern furnishings, and large windows make this a perfect base, it's lovely and peaceful.

- How many rooms are there? One, which sleeps two people.
- Mood? City life.
- Are there any location advantages? In the center of SoFo, a popular hangout for nice vibes and even amazing coffee.
- What is the budget range? Very reasonably priced.

8. The Isolated Home in Österåker

If you have more than two people, this beautiful lake home can accommodate nine. Bring your friends to this property with a lake plot in the middle of nowhere for a memorable holiday. The space is 95 square meters and about a mile away from Åkersberga. It has a fireplace, kitchen, and a wonderful lake view. There are two terraces and a BBQ, as well as a large grass, a rowing boat fishing place, and even a sauna. It sounds like the type of location you'd never want to leave, yet if you must, the sea is only 3 kilometers away.

- How many rooms are there? Three. Sleeps nine people.
- The mood is a lakeside luxury.
- Are there any location advantages? Live your best life in this lovely lakeside Airbnb with surrounding trees.
- What is the budget range? Offering in the mid-range yet with a premium feel.

9. The Eco-Friendly B&B Just Outside Of Town

If solar panels, lakeside saunas, and ecologically friendly materials pique your interest, make a beeline for this lovely B&B, which is nestled in an 'eco-village' with a natural reserve right on its doorstep. And, with the city only a 15-minute train trip away, it's simple to visit if you've had enough of the horrible fresh air.

- How many rooms are there? One, Sleeps two people.
- Mood? Green backpacker energy.

- Are there any location advantages? Nature and a feeling of community abound - and we're here to enjoy them.
- What is the budget range? Affordably priced for a room.

Stockholm Budget Hotels

1. Hotel Reimersholme

- **Address**: Reimersholmsgatan 5, 11740 Stockholm, Sweden

Reimersholme Hotel is located on Reimersholme Island in downtown Stockholm, surrounded by water, lovely architecture, and tranquil green areas. The Reimersholme Hotel is a vibrant establishment run by two Swedish artists. The pub hosts a variety of musical events, such as music quizzes and Karaoke evenings. There is also a wine bar in the restaurant with a large range of natural wines and amusing beers, as well as wonderful food with Swedish and French influences.

In a post-corona world, a smaller breakfast is provided upon request, and coffee is served at Hotel Reimersholme's lobby during business hours. During the summer, they changed their outside parking area into a massive beer park with a terrific continental ambiance for everyone to enjoy. The majority of rooms at Reimersholme Hotel contain an armchair or sofa, and some have a flat-screen TV. Bathrooms are either private or shared and offer a wide range of amenities and services.

Terms and Conditions for the Reimersholme Hotel:

- There is a 24-hour cancellation policy in place before arrival.
- Check-in hours are from 14:00 to 22:00.
- Check out by 11:00 a.m.
- Cash, credit cards, and debit cards accepted upon arrival; taxes included.
- Breakfast is provided.

General:

- Reception hours: Monday and Tuesday 7 a.m.-8 p.m., Wednesday-Friday 7 a.m.-4 p.m., Saturday and Sunday 8 a.m.-7 p.m.
- Check-in is also possible in the evenings from Wednesday to Sunday throughout our restaurant's operating hours. If you need to check in after hours, please call them and they will supply you with a self-check-in procedure.
- There is no curfew.
- No smoking is permitted.
- Age Restrictions: 18 and above only.

2. Ramilton Old Town Hostel

- **Location**: Stora Nygatan 22 in Stockholm, Sweden

Welcome to RAMILTON Old Town Hostel, Stockholm's newest hostel - totally restored premises set in a 17th-century subterranean vault. The Ramilton Old Town Hostel includes a common area, non-smoking rooms, and free WiFi. In the best position in Stockholm City, there is a fully equipped kitchen for visitors as well as a spacious community meeting space. They are at the core of Stockholm's arteries, a short distance from the castle,

Drottninggatan, and the ferries to Djurgården. They are a cutting-edge hostel built in the subterranean vault of the 17th-century Ehrencreutzka home. The rich surroundings add to the mystique, and the enormous ceiling height makes all 13 rooms appear quite big. There are two types of accommodations at the Old Town Hostel: quadruple and six-bed rooms. Every room has been completely renovated.

Policies and Terms

- Cancellation policy: 72 hours before arrival.
- Check-in hours are from 13:00 to 18:00.
- The hours of check-out are 5:00 to 11:00.
- Credit and debit cards are accepted upon arrival.
- Taxes are included.
- No breakfast is included.
- There is no curfew.

General:

- They do not accept consumers who are under the age of 18.
- No smoking is permitted.
- Bring your linens, but no sleeping bags.
- Rent sheets (one-time fee of SEK 100)
- 50 SEK towel rental
- Purchase a lock for 75 SEK.
- The multi-bed rooms do not include breakfast.
- They feature separate showers for men and women, as well as separate restrooms.
- The Old Town Hostel is built in a 17th-century subterranean vault; therefore there are no windows in the rooms.
- Prices are inclusive of VAT and subject to change.

3. Stockholm Inn Hotel

- **Address**: 67 Drottninggatan, Stockholm, Sweden

This is a recently constructed, contemporary, and economical lodging on Drottninggatan, in the heart of Stockholm. They provide you with a terrific location for a delightful stay in the Swedish capital, with the comfort of a hotel and the pricing of a property. Shopping, restaurants, and public transportation are all right outside your door. All of the rooms are brand new. Their inexpensive costs, central location, and high degree of comfort are ideal for anybody looking for a lovely and clean place to stay right in the heart of Stockholm.

Please Note:

- Cancellation policy: 72 hours advance notice
- One-night charge for late cancelation or no-show
- Credit cards (Visa or MasterCard) and cash are accepted upon arrival.
- Check in at 15.00
- Check out by 12.00
- Breakfast included
- Taxes included
- The entire property is non-smoking and we do not allow dogs

4. Dalagatan Hostel

- **Location**: Dalagatan 30 in Stockholm, Sweden

This hostel provides beautifully painted rooms near Vasaparken Park in downtown Stockholm. There is free Wi-Fi in the communal area. The Metro Station Odenplan is a 5-minute walk away. Hostel Dalagatan's soundproofed rooms include underfloor heating and either communal or private bathrooms. All rooms include the bed linen. Towels are only provided in the private rooms. In the fully equipped guest kitchen, guests may make meals and watch TV. The retail street Drottninggatan is 500 meters distant. Dalagatan Hostel is a 15-minute walk from Stockholm Central Station.

Please Keep in Mind:

- They Have A Non-Refundable Booking Policy!
- **Non-refundable**: If you cancel your booking, you will be charged the whole amount.
- **Prepayment**: The complete cost of the reservation will be paid after booking, and they only accept credit card payments. If your credit card is not valid, they retain the right to cancel your reservation. Payments, such as the deposit, are non-refundable in this circumstance.

Check-in Quickly:

- Once your reservation has been paid for and confirmed, you will get a single access code and room number via the email address associated with the booking.
- Bring your access code with you when you arrive!
- Check out by 11:00 a.m.
- No breakfast is included.
- There is no curfew.
- No smoking is permitted.
- Reception is open from 10 a.m. to 3 p.m.

- Guests under the age of 18 May only check in as part of a family trip.
- Please keep in mind that drinking and smoking are not permitted throughout the property.
- Final cleaning is included. Hostel Dalagatan does not provide daily cleaning.

5. Nomad Cave

- **Location**: 32 Hantverkargatan in Stockholm, Sweden.

Nomad Cave is a youth-oriented internet hostel located on the -1 floor. You can walk to all of the main tourist attractions. They have coded lockable rooms, baggage rooms, and access to the kitchen and laundry. They are an internet hostel with no reception. They take cleanliness seriously, therefore the rooms are fully cleaned after each visit, and a professional cleaning firm cleans the communal amenities daily.

How Does It Function?

- Reserve your room and pay in full in advance.
- Get room and bed numbers, as well as access credentials, within 24 hours of your arrival date.
- Fewest staff contacts!
- Dormitory in-room lockers with space for your padlock, common area with TV and free WiFi, baggage room with code, kitchenette with fridge, kettle, and microwave. The accommodation fee includes bed linen and one towel.

Group Discounts

- Are you planning a trip with friends or school? We have special discounts for parties of ten or more!
- Check-in/Check-out
- Check-in time is after 15.00. Simply enter the hostel using the codes!
- Check-out time: before 11 a.m. We have an express checkout: simply pack and leave.

Working Hours for Reception:

- 08:00 a.m. - 10:30 a.m. & 3:00 p.m. - 00:00 a.m.

Online Support Hours:

- Daily, from 07:00 a.m. to 11:00 p.m.

Payment:

- You are paying the entire payment at the time of booking. If your payment fails, they will send you an email with a receipt or notification.

Age Restrictions and Other Rules

- Children are welcome who are older than 12. Please keep in mind that we are not suited for children under the age of 12.
- Children under the age of 18 may remain at the hostel with their parents or legal guardians.
- No loud noise between 23.00 and 07.00
- No smoking, alcohol, or drug use or storage
- The hostel is not suited for wheelchair users owing to the technical building layout
- Maximum one-time stay is 14 days

Please note: we are a youth digital hostel for young backpacker travelers. All bookings are restricted to anyone aged 12 to 40.

Cancellation and No-Show Policies

- Free cancellation if you cancel at least 7 days before your arrival date. If you cancel less than 7 days before your arrival, they will charge you the whole price as a cancellation fee.

If you do not arrive for your stay without prior warning, you will be charged the whole price.

EXERCISE

With Your Travel Budget Where Do You Intend To Stay And How Was Your Experience?

_____
_____
_____
_____
_____
_____
_____
_____
_____
_____
_____
_____
_____
_____
_____
_____
_____
_____
_____
_____

CHAPTER SIX

The Best Boat Tours & Cruises in Stockholm

Stockholm is divided by 14 islands connected by winding canals and open waterways. No matter where you go in the city, you never seem to be far from the water.

Tours by boat in Stockholm

Ferries are an important element of the public transportation network since so many inhabitants travel from one island to another. There is also a bustling boat trip sector, with hundreds of colorful boats carrying tourists out onto the water to see the city from a new perspective. There are several boat tours available from Stockholm, with Lake Mälaren to the west and a wide archipelago to the east. Some take less than an hour, while others take considerably longer, allowing you to enjoy a full day of sun, sea, and sand. If you decide to take a boat cruise from Stockholm, there are a few things to consider.

The Best Type of Boat Tour

There are so many different boat trips and cruises to choose from that you may want to start restricting your selections early on. Finding out how much time you have available is the first step. A short tour of Stockholm's inner canals takes less than an hour, but a longer voyage to the Stockholm Archipelago takes at least three hours, if not the entire day.

The next step is to decide the path you wish to go on. Do you want to travel west towards Lake Mälaren, east past the city boundaries, or remain nice and center to get a sense of Stockholm's many neighborhoods from the water?

Another item to consider is the tour's substance. If you wish to experience Stockholm's sights from the water, hundreds of excursions circle the city's waterways and expose you to the city from the deck of a boat. If, on the other hand, you want to spend the day walking quaint alleys, eating wonderful kanelbullar (cinnamon buns), and soaking in magnificent panoramic views, you could visit one of the nearby archipelago islands, such as Vaxholm or Fjäderholmarna. If you want to learn more about Swedish history, take a boat trip to Lake Mälaren and visit Viking remains and 17th-century mansions.

Tips for a Stockholm Boat Tour

- Dress warmly and waterproof; it can get chilly even in the summer.
- Bring sunscreen with you throughout the summer (UV levels can be strong even in Sweden).
- Consider taking a private tour: sailing and kayaking are both choices.
- Just in case, bring cash and credit cards.
- Don't forget to bring your phone! You ought to snap a ton of photos.

Where Do The Boat Cruises Start?

There are harbors all across Stockholm, but if you're going on a boat excursion, chances are it'll leave from one in particular: Nybroviken in Norrmalm.

- There are three ports nearby: Nybroplan, Nybrokajen, and Strandvägen. Different trips leave from various piers.
- Strömkajen is another popular Norrmalm harbor. It is located at Södra Blasieholmshamnen 11. Many trips that stay inside the city borders, such as the Royal Canal Tour, begin here.
- Boats departing from Stockholm City Hall at Klara Mälarstrand 2 for Lake Mälaren, Drottningholm Palace, or Birka.
- Other departure points include Gustav Adolfs Torg (near the Opera House), Skeppsbron 2 (the Royal Palace), and Nacka Strand.

The departure places are constantly subject to change, so double-check your ticket to verify where your journey is leaving from.

Do the Boat Trips in Stockholm Continue All Year?

Summer (approximately April-September) is the peak season for boat trips in Stockholm, owing to the significantly warmer weather and the fact that the canals are now clear of ice. Some cruises and tours, such as the Royal Canal Tour, remain open for considerably longer, frequently until mid-December or whenever the water begins to freeze. Similarly, if the weather is pleasant and warm, trips may begin early in the spring. Tougher public boats travel all year to various locations of the Stockholm Archipelago. Of course, there are atmospheric winter excursions that run all year if there is no ice.

When Is The Ideal Time To Go On A Boat Trip In Stockholm?

There are advantages and disadvantages to taking a boat cruise at various times of the day. If you can get up early, the first trip of the day is frequently the quietest, and the rivers may be less crowded. However, it is also affected by the time of year. Boat rides are such a popular pastime in Stockholm that they may be crowded all day during the peak summer season. In the summer, taking a nighttime cruise when the rivers are quieter is an excellent option. Other activities take advantage of the long Swedish summer evenings, such as this evocative nighttime kayak tour that includes a BBQ.

When the mist rises off the lake and the trees are clothed in golden, crimson, and orange colors, autumn may be a great time to enjoy a boat ride. Winter on the river can also be incredibly evocative, with boats cruising by ice chunks and the city's roofs and pavements coated in snow. There are just a few trips like this one that runs in the winter, but those that do give blankets, hot beverages, and reindeer skins to keep the cold away.

Where Can I Get Tickets?

It is frequently less expensive and less trouble to book the ticket yourself. Tickets for all tours may be purchased online up to one hour before departure. After that, you may purchase tickets at Strömma's ticket offices at Strömkajen, Gustaf Adolfs Torg, Stadshusbron, and Nybroplan, or at tourist information centers. Some vessels, like the ferry to Vaxholm, allow you to board without a ticket and purchase one aboard.

Stockholm Passes

If you have a Stockholm Pass, a 'hop-on, hop-off' boat excursion, as well as a variety of additional boat tours and cruises, are included in the purchase of your pass in the summer.

18 Of Stockholm's Top Boat Trips and Cruises

Under the Bridges

Explore the center of Stockholm on this sightseeing cruise designed specifically for tourists. The trip, which passes beneath beautiful bridges, will take you to some of the city's most important attractions, with a recorded commentary accessible in ten languages. The 2-hour and 15-minute trip will take you from the Baltic Sea to Lake Mälaren, via bridges, and to the prominent sights of Södermalm, Stora Essingen, Hammarby Sjöstad, and woodland Djurgården.

1. Tour of the Royal Canal

Have less than an hour and want to catch a glimpse of Stockholm from the water? The Royal Canal Tour glides across the tranquil Djurgården canal, introducing you to the landscapes of this ancient island with an audio commentary in 11 languages. It's one of the busiest boat cruises available.

2. 'Hop-On, Hop-Off' Boat Tours

With the distinctive hop-on hop-off boat trip, you can see Stockholm at your leisure. Your boat ticket is good for 24 hours, allowing you to board and leave whenever you want: popular destinations include the Royal Palace, the Vasa Museum, Skansen, and the Abba Museum. If you're short on time, this is a great way to explore all of the city's key attractions.

3. Kayak around the Archipelago.

This enjoyable full-day kayak excursion takes you to the calmer regions of the archipelago. Glide down the coast, enjoy Stockholm from the sea, and explore the archipelago's smaller islands and rivers. Dry suits, lunch, hot drinks, and Swedish fika are all provided to keep you going while you paddle.

4. A trip to Vaxholm

Vaxholm is one of the archipelago's most popular islands, with a charming village, narrow alleyways, shops, galleries, and the 16th-century Vaxholm fortress. You have two options for getting there: a speedy boat that takes around fifty minutes or an atmospheric antique wooden boat that takes approximately 90 minutes. In either case, you could easily spend a whole day visiting Vaxholm before returning to Stockholm.

5. Restaurant cruises from Stockholm

A dining cruise is ideal if you want to relax and enjoy a nice meal on Stockholm's beautiful canals rather than sightsee. Brunch, lunch, and dinner cruises are available, as well as a buffet evening cruise with live music.

There's even a 'shrimp boat,' a three-hour sunset cruise of the archipelago that includes all-you-can-eat shrimp.

6. Fjäderholmarna Offers A Glimpse Of Island Life.

Visit Fjäderholmarna, the archipelago islands nearest to Stockholm. Glassblowers, smiths, potters, and stores offering artisan goods may all be found here. It's only a 30-minute boat ride there, so spend the day relaxing and catching the boat back before it gets too dark (about 10 p.m. in the summer!). The boat ride to Fjäderholmarna is included with a Stockholm Pass.

7. At Birka, You May Learn About History.

Birka, a once-thriving Viking village dating back to the 750s, will appeal to history buffs. It is the first city in Sweden and a fascinating Unesco World Heritage Site. You may explore the Viking remains and open-air museum as much as you like, and then eat real Viking meals cooked from locally sourced ingredients at the themed Särimner Restaurant (open from May to October).

8. Drottningholm Palace Should Be Visited.

Drottningholm Palace, the Royal Family's house and a Unesco World Heritage Site, is another popular stop for Lake Mälaren cruises. If you've come this far, you should see its lovely parks, manicured gardens, ancient theater, and Chinese pavilion. You may purchase a combo ticket that covers both the one-hour boat excursion and admission to the royal grounds. Alternatively, you can purchase a return boat ticket or go one-way by boat and return by metro.

If you have a Stockholm Pass, the boat ride to Drottningholm is complimentary, so you just need to purchase your admission ticket to the palace.

9. Tour via Amphibious Bus

Here's a unique way to experience the city via land and sea. The Ocean Bus amphibious bus tour begins with a trip through Stockholm's historic center before going to the water and experiencing the city's wonders from the sea. Once on the water, the ten-tonne amphibious bus travels by the Vasa Museum and the islands of Södermalm and Skeppsholmen, from where the Royal Palace may be seen.

10. Kayak around Lake Mälaren.

This full-day guided kayak excursion takes you around Lake Mälaren, past the magnificent Steninge Palace, the regal Rosersberg Palace, and the iron-age village of Runsa. You'll explore the old village of Sigtuna after kayaking roughly 12 kilometers and stopping for a picnic lunch on a desolate island.

11. Winter cruise in Stockholm

Even if the weather is awful, you can still go on a boat excursion. Indeed, viewing Stockholm from the lake, with its buildings coated in snow and ice on the shoreline, is more evocative than seeing it in the summer. You won't get chilly since reindeer skins are provided, and warming bowls of traditional Swedish pea soup and hot glögg (mulled wine) may be purchased on board.

12. Sail Around Stockholm's Archipelago.

Spend the day sailing around a handful of the 24,000 islands that make up the Stockholm archipelago. A professional skipper will take you around some of the less-visited and isolated islands, and you may even try your hand at directing and crewing the boat yourself. On-board refreshments and a Swedish lunch are provided.

13. Travel via boat to Djurgården Island.

This guided tour of Stockholm's top attractions includes a ferry ride over to the island of Djurgården. You'll walk about the old town and learn about its history before boarding a boat to Djurgården and viewing the famous Vasa ships museum.

14. Take A Rib Tour Of The Archipelago.

This hour-long tour of the archipelago takes you as far out as Fjäderholmarnas. You'll view the attractions of Stockholm from the sea before hitting speeds of up to 40 miles per hour as you travel out to the Baltic Sea's more remote islands.

15. Take A Live Music Eco-Boat Cruise.

On an environmentally friendly electric boat, this enjoyable early-evening cruise glides among the city's canals and beneath its bridges. There will be live musicians on board to entertain you as you float by the city's sites and rivers. You are welcome to bring your food and beverages to enhance the party's mood.

16. In a massive boat, explore the Bogesund Nature Reserve.

It may sound strange, but you can even explore the archipelago in a 15-person boat. This tour departs from the island of Vaxholm and takes you out into the tranquil seas of a nature reserve, making it ideal for large parties or lone travelers eager to meet new folks and have some fun. While kayaking, keep an eye out for seals, beavers, and deer.

17. Kayak A Sunset Barbecue Tour.

This enjoyable evening kayak trip departs from Stockholm's Langholmen Island at 6 p.m. and paddles around the city's waterways for an hour before docking for a delicious supper. You may swim while your guide prepares the BBQ, and then enjoy the sunset as you paddle back.

18. Helsinki Boat Cruises

Why not take this three-day mini-cruise to Finland from Stockholm for the ultimate boat trip? You'll spend two nights aboard the boat, with a buffet breakfast included, and six hours on land touring Helsinki, Finland's intriguing city. As you arrive and depart, you get fantastic vistas of both cities, plus there are restaurants, karaoke, and even a spa on board.

Tours by Private Boat

And if you want to splurge on a truly unique way to see the Stockholm Archipelago, why not rent your private yacht for you and your friends or family? This three-hour yacht hire for up to six people includes your own fully certified captain as well as onboard lunch or supper. You may also select where to travel and which islands to visit because you are in command.

What to Bring on a Boat Tour

Of course, what you need to bring depends on the time of year and the sort of boat excursion you've selected. However, here is a rough list of items you may need to bring.

- **Dress in layers.** The weather is famously unpredictable, so even if it's nice when you go, it might turn extremely chilly on the water. In contrast, if the sun comes out in the summer, you'll be fast removing your sweaters.

- **A sunscreen**. Even if it's foggy when you go, carry sunscreen because the sun may be harsh in the summer and is exaggerated by the water.

- **Waterproofing**. You won't need these on a large boat, but carry waterproof gear if you're kayaking or canoeing.

- **Snacks and water.** Again, huge boats frequently sell food and beverages, but if you're on a tight budget or kayaking, bring your own.

- **A camera or phone**. Stockholm is breathtakingly beautiful, and you don't want to miss out on any of the photo opportunities!

- **Money**. Check to see whether food and drink are included on your trip, and if not, bring your credit card or phone (cash is rarely accepted). Some of the larger boats frequently provide the option to purchase food and beverages on board.

DID YOU SMILE TODAY?

EXECRCISE

With The Boat Tours And Cruises In Shockholm, Which Of The Boat Trips Do You Intend To Take?

_____
_____
_____
_____
_____
_____
_____
_____

What Are Your Experiences With The Tours?

_____
_____
_____
_____
_____
_____
_____
_____

CHAPTER SEVEN

The Top 8 Hikes in Stockholm

Swedes have an active, healthy lifestyle and like spending time outside, and breathing in fresh air. Hiking in the deep forests close to Stockholm is a popular pastime among both residents and visitors. Trekking routes winding through the countryside are accessible for hikers of all skill levels, and you may walk for an hour or spend a few days trekking and communing with nature. Make a weekend of exploring Stockholm's greatest hikes with your pals. Have you brought the kids? This is a fantastic exercise for kids. Take on some of the smaller, gentler hikes while teaching your children about the local flora and animals. You might wish to go on your own for a tranquil hike to clear your head and awaken your senses.

Before you hit the trail, store any excess baggage in a luggage storage locker in Stockholm. Make a map and a plan so you know precisely where you're going to trek and how long you'll be there. Bring a supply bag that includes water, a first-aid kit, food, and any other little essentials you may require.

Stockholm's Best Hiking Trails

You may explore a multitude of hiking paths in and around Stockholm. Here are just a few examples of the incredible sites and trails you may visit. Each one is great in its unique way.

1. **Roslagsleden**

The Baltic Coast has 118 miles of hiking paths, making it one of the most popular hiking destinations around Stockholm. Roslagsleden is divided into 11 parts, each with beautiful sights. To reach there from Stockholm City Centre, use Line 14 of the T-Centralen in downtown Stockholm and exit at Morby Centrum. Then it's only a 15-minute walk to Danderyd Church, where you'll discover the path. The trail is well-marked, with orange paint on trees and other landmarks. The entire path runs through Domarudden, Norrtalje, Roslagsbro, and Grisslehamn.

You may trek for an hour, all day, or spend the night at one of the campgrounds. If you wish to spend the night in luxury after a hard day of trekking, there are B&Bs and motels along the path. Along the trip, you'll visit medieval cathedrals, Viking rune stones, historical castles, and even crystal-clear lakes. If you can only view specific parts of Roslagsleden, there are three sections you must not miss. Angarnssjoangen in section two is a great area to go bird viewing. Wira Bruk's sections 5 and 6 are densely packed with historical red homes and medieval churches. Section 11 is home to Swedish novelist and artist Albert Engstrom's studio, which overlooks the Sea of Aland.

2. Nackareservatet

The Nacka Nature Reserve, or Nackareservatet, is one of 12 nature reserves on the island of Nacka and is only about 30 minutes from Stockholm's city center. The T-Bana 17 from Stockholm Central Station to Bagarmossen gets you within a few minutes of the reserve. Several pathways are suitable for hikers of various levels. Everyone may have a good day at Nackareservatet, from beginners to expert hikers. Birdwatchers like meandering through the area in search of as many birds as possible. There are also several lakes in the region where you can swim. Stockholm Adventures may take you on a guided trek or provide information on self-directed hikes. With the natural reserve being so near to the city, one would expect to see and hear rush and activity, yet the walk is peaceful and quiet.

3. National Park of Tyresta

This is yet another wonderful set of hiking trails about 40 minutes from Stockholm. This national park is one of Sweden's greatest assets. To reach the park, take the 807 or 809 bus from Gullmarsplan station or the 834 bus from Haninge station into Tyresta. The Tyresta National Park is one of Sweden's largest woods. The virgin forest has not been harmed, and it was designated a national park in 1993. Make a day of it by bringing a picnic and spending time outside in the fresh air. There are paths for all ability levels to select from. The Barnvagnsslingan loop is a three-mile easy trek that is around Bylsjon Lake. Along the Barnvagnsslingan loop, you can even carry a strong stroller.

If you're looking for a challenge, follow the orange trail markers and enter the Sormlandsleden route. This portion is around eight miles long and will take you approximately five hours to finish. The difficult terrain is a workout, but it is so wonderful when you finish it. Pack a bag with lots of water, food, and a first-aid kit. Tyresta has a café for refreshments as well as an intriguing farm shop. Several of the city's structures are from the 18th and 19th centuries. The Naturum is another thing you should not miss. It is a structure in the shape of a map of Sweden composed primarily of eco-friendly and natural materials.

4. Lake Brunnsviken

The Brunnsviken Lake walk, which round the lake for seven miles, is one of the greatest family-friendly hiking trails in Stockholm. The walk is level and loaded with intriguing objects that will keep most children's attention. Pack a picnic and spend a beautiful afternoon stretching your legs along the lake's edge. Take the T-Bana 14 to Universitetet, then a short walk to Brunnsviken Lake. A butterfly house, the Bergius Botanic Garden, and the Swedish Museum of Natural History (one of Stockholm's fantastic museums) are all within walking distance. You should also view King Gustav III's grandiose pavilion before returning to Stockholm and stopping at Kafé Sjostugan for one of their famed cinnamon pastries.

5. Jarvafaltet, Norra

Norra Jarvafaltet, located just north of Stockholm, is home to four nature reserves and encompasses about 4,700 acres of meadows, lakes, and woodlands. You may take the T-Bana Line 11 into Akalla and walk to Hansta to join one of the trails there, or you can take the 567 bus into Saby Gard and join various paths that meander through the natural reserves. Several routes will lead you past Bronze Age remains such as burial mounds and forts. If you enjoy bird watching, go to Getholmen Island and visit the bird sanctuary. Keep in mind that the sanctuary is closed from April to June.

6. Sormlandsleden

This path was briefly mentioned in Tyresta National Park, where a segment may be visited, however, Sormlandsleden is one of the longest trails in Scandinavia, not simply Sweden. With over 621 miles to travel, relatively few visitors to Stockholm hike the full path. The trailhead is conveniently located in the City Centre; simply take the T-Centralen Metro Line 17 to the Bjorkhagen stop. Then go to the path, which is separated into over 100 hiking trails. Hikers of various abilities may choose which one they want to tackle. Trails range in length from one mile to eleven miles.

One of the paths passes through Skottvang, a historic mining town. You'll walk along routes that follow coastlines, around beautiful lakes, and through floral fields. You could even spot a roe deer or moose, as well as an eagle or two swooping over. If you intend on trekking some of the lengthier parts, Sormlandsleden will take you through various villages. While trekking the Sormlandsleden, you might stop in Oxelosund, Eskilstuna, Nynashamn, Nykoping, Sodertalje, and Trosa.

7. Upplandsleden

The Uppland Trail is one of the greatest hiking paths around Stockholm, with sleeping cabins, rest places, and firepits along the way for those who want to stay overnight. The sleeping cabins are free and available on a first-come, first-served basis. The path is designed for intermediate hikers and is separated into portions ranging from 3 to 19 miles. Hike through marshes, old woodlands, and along rocky coastlines. When seeking a pleasant day excursion, the four-mile trek at Lanna or the five-mile hike at Sunnersta Asen will take you into the forest and is another fantastic day trip. Upplandsleden has 14 loop routes for people searching for a short but tough walk. If you're feeling ambitious, you may climb the 310 kilometers from Malardalen Bay to the Dalalven archipelago, which would take many weeks. Kolarmoraan in section nine is a popular path where you may paddle down the river if you want to take a break from trekking. Farnebofjarden National Park in sections 18-20 is another popular walk with little islands and sandy shoreline. Both locations are ideal for birding or looking for local animals.

8. Malarolederna

A remarkable network of hiking routes winding around a few islands on Lake Malaren. The Malaroarna hiking paths are great fun for hikers of all ability levels and a great opportunity to go out and appreciate nature while in Stockholm. The Lovo hiking trail winds through the Lovo Nature Reserve, past beaches, and into the woods. This 11-mile track takes you straight past Drottningholm Palace. The Adelso hiking route is 9.9 miles long and will take you past ancient tombs as well as an observation tower from where you can witness spectacular views of Lake Malaren. The Ekero-Munso hiking track then leads you on an 11-mile excursion into Skytteholm, where a golf club and hotel await. The second section of the Ekero-Munso path is nine miles long and provides various opportunities to cool off and swim in the cool, clear water.

Simple Hikes in Stockholm

There are various easy treks available for novices or those seeking a pleasant stroll through a natural preserve. Consider visiting Malarolederna, Upplandsleden, and Tyresta National Park. The paths are not usually labeled with their difficulty levels, but you can always use the AllTrails app or the visitors' center for additional information.

Stockholm Intermediate Hikes

You will find plenty to keep you busy in the great outdoors, whether you are wandering through national parks or challenging yourself with a seaside stroll. Take your rucksack, lace up your hiking boots, and explore some of these suggested paths. Tyresta National Park, Roslagsleden, and Upplandsleden are excellent locations for moderate to strenuous exercise. After that, treat your company to breakfast in Stockholm!

Hikes in Stockholm That Are Difficult

Experienced hikers will find plenty of paths to test them in and around Stockholm. The sheer splendor of the outdoors will take your breath away as you travel through nature reserves and national parks. Check out the spectacular challenging walks Roslagsleden, Sormlandsleden, and Malarolederna.

Hiking Trails in Stockholm

With so many fantastic hiking paths, you'll never be bored. The trail runs through pine forests and along the Baltic Sea and will take your breath away. Sweden's Baltic Coast is one of the best areas to hike, with everything from basic routes to more difficult hikes for expert hikers; Stockholm is the place to trek!

EXERCISE

Do You Intend To Hike, If Yes Where Is Your Target Area?

CHAPTER EIGHT

Making the Most of Family Adventures When Traveling with Children

Traveling with children may be one of the most enjoyable experiences, despite the challenges. Family trips strengthen bonds between parents and children and assist in building lasting memories. Traveling with children, however, requires a different technique than solo or adult group travel. Here are some ideas for making the most of family excursions.

1. Destination Planning

Choosing the proper place for a family trip is critical. Consider sites that provide a variety of amusements and activities that appeal to youngsters and adults. Look for places that provide family-friendly attractions, such as interactive exhibitions, theme parks, and museums. Consider visiting cities that provide hop-on, hop-off bus excursions so you can see the sights without getting lost.

2. Preparing for the Journey

Preparing for a family vacation entails more than simply packing your suitcase. It is critical to plan ahead of time for a pleasant voyage. Make a list of what to carry for each family member, including essentials such as travel papers, food, and prescription medicines. Do some research to find out what amenities are available at your location and what you need to carry. Before going on a foreign vacation, make sure everyone's passports are up to date, and include a universal travel adaptor.

3. Keeping Children Amused

One of the most difficult aspects of traveling with children is keeping youngsters entertained during long flights or car rides. Bring a variety of games and activities to keep the kids occupied. Consider taking a tablet or e-reader loaded with games, movies, and reading. Bring a few beloved toys and soft animals for the younger kids. Consider taking a hop-on, hop-off bus tour to keep the youngsters entertained while you explore your location.

4. Planning a Family Vacation Budget

There are methods to keep costs down while traveling with children, but they may be expensive. Find kid-friendly sites, such as parks, beaches, and museums that provide free or low-cost activities. Consider renting a hotel or vacation rental that has amenities such as complimentary breakfast or kitchenettes for cooking. When visiting a new city, take advantage of hop-on, hop-off bus tours that give inexpensive transportation and sightseeing.

5. Considerations for Safety

When traveling with children, safety is of the utmost importance. Do some research about the location you're traveling to to learn about any hazards or safety problems. Consider purchasing trip cancelation and medical travel insurance. Make sure that everyone in the family knows what to do and who to call in an emergency. Consider using a GPS tracker or a family locator app to keep track of each other's locations.

6. Making Long-lasting Memories

The purpose of family travel is to create lasting experiences that will be enjoyed for years to come. Take multiple photographs and videos to capture those memorable moments. Consider creating a travel diary or scrapbook to document your travels. When visiting a new city, take a hop-on, hop-off bus tour to see the sights and create family memories.

Traveling with children may be enjoyable and beneficial for the entire family. By choosing the right venue, planning ahead of time, amusing the kids, managing your money wisely, and being safe, you may create lasting memories that will be remembered for years to come. Taking a hop on hop off bus excursion allows you to quickly visit the sights and discover new areas.

Stockholm's Best Family-Friendly Locations

Stockholm is a fantastic destination for families. It is instantly seen in the architecture of municipal parks and civic buildings, children's menus in restaurants, and child care on public transportation. Sweden is one of the greatest family vacation locations in Europe for these and other reasons. Many of Stockholm's top family attractions are on the island of Djurgården in the city's west, but getting around is easy owing to the superb public transportation system. If you have a stroller, you may ride public buses for free. Furthermore, most attractions, museums, and events admit small children for free.

1. Open-Air Museum Skansen

Travel through 5 centuries of pre-industrialized Sweden.

Skansen is a living history museum that depicts how Swedes used to live. You may visit farmsteads and craft stores, enjoy traditional cuisine, and pet the animals. Skansen is a full-scale reproduction of an ancient village that spans 300,000 square meters. Some of the things made here are even for sale.

Skansen commemorates seasonal festivals such as Midsummer, Harvest time, and New Year's Eve throughout the year by traditional customs. It's an intriguing approach to learning about Sweden's old culture.

- **Address**: Djurgårdsslätten 49-51, Stockholm, Sweden (115 21).

- Open every day at 10 a.m. (closing times change during the year)
- **Phone**: +46 (0)8-442 82 00

2. Lund, Gröna

Rides the rollercoasters and gets scared in the scary home.

Gröna Lund is a retro theme park with unexpectedly quick and thrilling rides. The park, which is located on Djurgården Island, offers over 30 attractions ranging from bumper cars to vertical freefall roller coasters. The walk-through haunted home is scary if you appreciate a good scare - you've been warned! Teens will like Gröna Lund amusement park, which is free for children under the age of six. Gröna Lund is also a prominent live music venue, hosting many of the world's best performers during the summer. For more information, see their website.

- **Address**: 9 Lilla Allmänna Gränd, 115 21 Stockholm, Sweden
- Open from May to September (hours vary)
- **Phone**: +46 (0)10 708 91 00

3. Tanto Strandbad Is A Great Place To Unwind On The Beach.

In the summer, jump into the Baltic Sea.

Stockholm features many beaches in the city center, all of which are crowded during the summer. Tanto Strandbad is a popular swimming location for families. People camp on the rocky beach or in the meadow behind the excellent sandy areas, which fill up rapidly. It is wheelchair accessible and includes public showers. You may spend the entire day here on Södermalm Island, enjoying the beach before moving to adjacent Tantolunden Park to play on the playground or play mini golf.

- **Location**: Tanto Strandbad is located at Skarpskyttestigen 6, 117 41 Stockholm, Sweden.

4. Department store Åhléns City

The fourth floor is reserved for children.

Åhléns is a popular department store in Sweden, having many locations in Stockholm. The main shop and the most convenient for tourists is Åhléns City. It is connected to T-Centralen station and is usually crowded. This four-story shop is a hidden gem for families. The mall's eateries and coffee shops are all kid-friendly, making it a quick and simple alternative for meal times. On the upper level, there is also a well-equipped family room. The whole children's section has been created with bright colors, quirky furnishings, and interactive elements in mind.

- **Address**: Klarabergsgatan 50, Stockholm, Sweden (111 21).
- **Operating hours**: 10 a.m. to 9 p.m., Monday through Friday., Saturday, 10 a.m. to 7 p.m., and Sunday, 11 a.m. to 7
- **Phone**: +46 (0)8 676 60 00

5. Spelmuseum in Stockholm

At Stockholm's Video Game Museum, you may play Pac-Man and other games.

The Spelmuseum in Stockholm is a modest but entertaining museum dedicated to the history of video game consoles. It shows vintage Nintendo and Atari computers and allows you to play retro games. The museum's collection of 1980s arcade games, such as Pac-Man and Space Invaders, is a highlight. A VR station, which brings things solidly into the twenty-first century, allowing you to witness how the game industry has grown over the previous few decades. Stockholms Spelmuseum is a private museum that is the proprietors' labor of love. Admittance is free for children under five.

- **Address**: 2 Markvardsgatan, 113 53 Stockholm, Sweden
- Open from 12 a.m. to 6 p.m. on Fridays and Thursdays, from 10 a.m. to 4 p.m. on Saturdays and Sundays.

6. Livrustkammaren

Livrustkammaren, or the Royal Armoury, is Sweden's oldest museum. It began as a venue for the monarch to show his armor in the 1600s and evolved from there. Some of the items on the exhibit are blood-splattered and have battle scars, which add to the realism. There's even a tour for kids that explains renowned princess and knight stories through costumes, games, and goodies. It is free to access and is located in the Royal Palace's basement.

- **Location**: Slottsbacken 3, 111-30 Stockholm, Sweden
- **Open**: Tuesday through Sunday, 11 a.m. to 5 p.m. (extended hours on Thursdays)

7. The Tekniska Museet

The Swedish National Museum of Science and Technology includes a lot of activities for kids. Indeed, the majority of the exhibitions are geared toward children. Highlights include MegaMind, which allows you to conduct fascinating things like paint on a computer screen using only your eyeballs and generate music by moving your body. These are only two of the numerous interactive exhibitions available. The museum also has an amazing model railway from the 1950s and a duplicate mine that exhibits how laborers used to work underground using technology.

- **Address**: 7 Museivägen, 115 27 Stockholm, Sweden
- **Hours of operation**: daily from 10 a.m. to 5 p.m. (open till 8 p.m. on Wednesdays)

8. Junibacken

This children's attraction focuses on bringing to life well-known Swedish literary characters. You may play in Pippi Longstocking's house, ride the Story Train, and see live theater adaptations of children's stories. Despite its diminutive size, Junibacken will fascinate children aged 4 to 8. Entry fees vary by age and start at 150 kr. Admittance is free for children under two. The museum is located on Djurgården Island and is flanked by several other family-friendly activities, so you could easily spend the entire day there.

- The address is Galärvarvsvägen 8, 115 21 Stockholm, Sweden.
- **Open**: Hours of operation vary greatly. It's normally open from 10 a.m. to 5 p.m. but check their website beforehand.
- **Phone**: +46 (0)8 587 230 00

9. Eriksdalsbadet

Eriksdalsbadet is a huge swimming pool complex comprising indoor and outdoor pools, two fun slides, a separate child pool, and hot pools. There is plenty of room for those who want to play in the water without upsetting others who want to swim laps. Swimming in the outdoor heated pool in the middle of winter is a lovely experience. There's also a sauna and a gym. It is located in the southern part of Sodermalm, near the Metro and tram connections. This is a popular place all year, especially with families.

- **Hours of operation**: daily from 6 a.m. to 6 p.m. (extended hours from Sunday to Thursday)
- **Phone**: +46 (0)8 508 402 58

10. The Stadsteatern Kulturhuset

Kulturhuset Stadsteatern is a massive facility that supports a wide range of arts, including theater, dance, cinema, music, literature, and debate. The building's design is a superb example of Nordic architecture, and with 8 unique stages, there are lots of intriguing events happening all year. Family-friendly performances may be given in either Swedish or English. Go to the top level for a great view of the center of Stockholm.

- **Location**: Sergels torg, 111 57 Stockholm, Sweden.
- Operating hours are 9 a.m. to 7 p.m., Monday through Friday, and 11 a.m. to 5 p.m. on weekends.
- **Phone**: +46 (0)8 506 202 12

Activities for Children in Stockholm

Visiting Stockholm with children may be both tough and enjoyable. It's difficult because you have to keep them occupied and guarantee that they enjoy their time as much as you do. Whether you reside here or want to make the most of the school vacations, you'll want to provide kids with memorable experiences. The good news is that Sweden's capital is a fantastic family destination. There are many enjoyable activities to do in Stockholm with kids, as well as many family adventures to keep your children entertained. You may play mini golf together, swim in outdoor pools in the summer, ride roller coasters, or view Nordic creatures at the zoo. If you're traveling with older children, they'll be amazed by the scientific museums, historical structures, and art galleries in Stockholm, as well as the distinctive Swedish history.

Take them to Stockholm Central Station so they can view the underground and trains. If you're planning a day trip from Stockholm, here is the ideal place to start. It's one of the most inviting locations in Sweden, and no matter how many times you visit; you'll fall in love with it. Aside from many intriguing activities, it also offers a dependable public transportation system, making it simple to go around and explore the city center and beyond with your children.

Junibacken Transports You to a Fairytale World

Junibacken is a one-of-a-kind museum in Stockholm that offers your children a variety of activities, such as dressing up and meeting characters from Astrid Lindgren's novels, riding the tale train, and more. You'll become engrossed in the fairy stories included in children's books. It's an excellent approach to introduce your children to museums! There's also no better spot to spend the weekend with the whole family than within Sweden's largest Moomin playground. Allow your children to play in the big snail and slide from the six-meter-tall playhouse. If you and your children need to refuel, you may stop at the restaurant and eat some traditional prepared cuisine. This amusement park is located in Djurgården, behind the Nordic Museum and a short walk from the Vasa Museum.

Skansen Open-air Museum is a great place to learn about history and see animals.

When visiting Stockholm with your family, Skansen is a wonderful choice. It is the world's oldest open-air museum, showcasing the country's history and farming culture from all around Sweden. It's an amazing site where history meets modernity and craftsmanship thrives.

Allow your children to take a journey down memory lane and learn about their ancestors' lives. Younger children will enjoy the playgrounds and the Children's Zoo, which has many little animals and play spaces. They can observe the animals, ride the attractions, and play with vintage toys. A classroom with interactive educational tools is also available at the zoo.

Gröna Lund Offers Thrilling Rides.

Visiting an amusement park is without a doubt one of the top things to do in Stockholm with kids. Gröna Lund, founded in 1883 on the western bank of Djurgården Island, is the country's oldest amusement park. It is heavily packed with adventures, rides, and other attractions in a space of fewer than five hectares. Gröna Lund is proud of its original fair atmosphere in a beautiful setting with a panoramic view of the city. Aside from the rides, there are modest food and candy stands, restaurants, lottery booths, and a variety of games.

Take A Stroll In Gamla Stan.

After participating in a variety of exciting activities in the city, you may find yourself stranded and unsure of how to delight your older children. In such a scenario, go to Gamla Stan, or the Old Town, Stockholm's oldest neighborhood. It is home to several historical sites, such as the Museum of Medieval Stockholm, the Royal Palace, the National Swedish Opera House, and others. You don't have to go inside those buildings; instead, take a stroll along the cobblestone streets and see what the neighborhood has to offer. Stop by Stortorget, Stockholm's Grand Square, and get a typical Swedish sausage from one of the square's hot dog kiosks. It's a fantastic opportunity to get to know gorgeous Stockholm while also learning about its culture and history. If you're not sure where to stay in Stockholm, Gamla Stan is a good option.

Visit the Vasa Museum to see the Salvaged Ship.

Anyone, regardless of age, is attracted by ships, which is why Vasa Museum is one of the greatest free things to do in Stockholm with kids. Yes, there is an entrance price; however, children and young adults under the age of 18 are admitted for free. It's a popular museum in Scandinavia, including a well-preserved battleship from 1628 that sank on its inaugural trip. There's also a garden with plants and flowers from the time of the Swedish ships. The story of King Gustavus Adolphus' ship would be an excellent one to tell your children. If you need a break from your activities, stop into the Vasa Museum Restaurant to quench your hunger and refresh your batteries.

At The Royal Armoury, You May Learn About Royal Life.

The Royal Armoury is located in Stockholm's Old Town in the Royal Palace, the official house of the Swedish monarch. It displays glittering vehicles and spectacular costumes from the country's royal past. It is Sweden's oldest museum, including weaponry and ceremonial equipment from royal weddings, coronations, and funerals. If you go to the children's room, you'll encounter a magical world full of activities and games. You may play, sketch, and try on knight costumes and clothing. The nicest aspect of visiting this museum is that you can learn about history, arts, and culture for free.

At The Stockholm Toy Museum, You May Play With Classic Toys.

When taking children to a museum, it may be challenging to strike a balance between enjoyment and learning. If you're having trouble with this, take your kids to the Stockholm Toy Museum.

The most extensive collection of toys and comics in Northern Europe may be found at Skeppsholmen, Stockholm. This Toy Museum is an ideal gathering spot for children and children at heart. Adults will be charmed by the ancient toys dating back to the 15th century. Grandmas and grandpas will experience nostalgia when they discover several of their favorite toys from their childhood.

The National Science and Technology Museum

The largest technological museum in Sweden provides some of the top things to do in Stockholm with kids. It covers about 10,000 square meters and attracts over 350,000 visitors each year on average. With exhibits such as 100 Innovations and Mega Mind, you and your children will be blown away by everything science and technology. Zero Cities is one of Tekniska's biggest attractions. Adults and children may work together to design a future metropolis that is free of fossil fuels and kind to the environment. The collection of the National Museum of Science and Technology includes around 800 audio recordings, 400 films, and 700 video cassettes.

Photograph inside the Milajki Style FactOH!Ry

Do you know what a selfie museum is? Inside Milajki Style FactOH!, you and your children will have a one-of-a-kind experience. It's the country's first pop-up selfie museum, with a wealth of entertaining activities to enjoy among the brilliant colors and photo-friendly settings. Allow your children to experience the selfie museum's creative spaces every day from 10 a.m. to 8 p.m. Enter picture booths with themes such as freakshows, unicorns, and disco wave mermaids. Milajki Style FactOH!'s enticing and memorable word Sergelgatan 2 has Ry waiting for you.

Sprvägsmuséet Transports You To The Past.

The popular children's museum Sprvägsmuseet, or The Transport Museum, is reopening its doors after a five-year absence. This year is the museum's 100th anniversary, so expect some mind-blowing activities. Bring your children to view artifacts and activities that demonstrate the function of public transportation and how it has affected people's lives for over 150 years. Sprvägsmuseet is open from 11 a.m. to 7 p.m., Tuesday through Sunday. This is one of the free things to do in Stockholm with kids if you are a member of any museum association. It encourages educational visits so that children may experience the museum's almost 70 cars, 20,000 drawings, and 10,000 other things. The museum is located in Norra Djurgårdsstaden Gasworks District.

Take them to Äventyrsbanan in Stockholm.

It's time to put your entire family to the test at a Stockholm adventure park. Äventyrsbanan, located in Älta to the south of Nacka's beautiful natural reserve, provides demanding rope courses in an unrivaled location. It's great for adults, but it's also one of the finest things to do in Stockholm with kids, especially if you want them to be more physically active. Aside from the rope courses, it also has one of Stockholm's longest and fastest ziplines, making it ideal for families. Once the courses are finished, they provide everyone with an inner challenge, plenty of fresh air, and a sense of success.

The Antiquities Museum of Gustav III

Gustav III's Museum of Antiquities is another museum situated within the Stockholm Royal Palace. Inside this museum, several attractions reflect the colorful life of the former Swedish monarch. Inside Gustav III's Museum of Antiquities, you'll find a fantastic collection of antiquities ranging from stone galleries to classical paintings. Over 200 sculptures will transport the children back in time. The exhibition hall will be welcomed by two stone galleries with a magnificent view of the Logården or "Shot Yard." Gustav III's Museum of Antiquities, one of Europe's oldest museums, is open from May to September each year.

See the Treasury's Priceless Treasures.

Introduce the kids to the most valuable objects in Swedish history inside The Treasury, one of Stockholm Palace's museums. The Regalia are housed inside The Treasury, one of Stockholm Palace's museums. Made by Jürgen Dargema in 1650, the Regalia were given to the King or Queen at the coronation. The oldest object preserved inside The Treasury's inner sanctuary is the two swords of state belonging to Gustav Vasa.

Visit the Tre Kronor Museum.

The remains of a 13th-century defensive wall and other artifacts await children and adults alike inside Museum Tre Kronor or Museum Three Crowns. The wooden blockade built by Vikings in the 900s is one of the most popular features of this interactive museum.

Actual objects and models rescued from the fire of 1697 in the original Tre Kronor Palace in Stockholm are also displayed.

The Nobel Prize Museum Is A Sight To Behold.

Inside the Nobel Prize Museum, children can be inspired by the milestones and achievements of famous people. The Nobel Prize Museum aims to spread knowledge of natural sciences and culture, particularly among children. It is located in the former Stock Exchange Building and presents information about the Nobel Prize, including its founder Alfred Nobel, and all the winners of the world's most coveted prize.

Stockholm with Children

There's no shortage of fun things to do in Stockholm with kids, no matter which part of the city you explore or what time of year you visit. While some main attractions are specifically aimed at young children, others are designed to keep the entire family entertained, including the kids and the kids at heart.

EXERCISE

How Do You Wish To Make The Most Of Your Trip If You're Traveling with Children And Hope The Guide Is Helpful In Doing That?

_____
_____
_____
_____
_____
_____
_____
_____
_____
_____

Is The Above Mention Family Friendly Location Worth It, Or You Have Other Options?

_____
_____
_____
_____

Making The Most Memorable Trip With Your Kids, Is The Guide Helpful With Fun Activities?

CHAPTER NINE

Stockholm's Best Lakes and Beaches

Stockholm has no shortage of natural beauty, and no vacation to the Swedish capital would be complete without a visit to one of the city's top lakes or beaches. There are open-air swimming locations along shallow beaches that are ideal for kids, as well as craggier outcrops where couples may have a romantic picnic in the evening light. If you want to do something other than relax, various locations offer pulse-raising activities and workout paths. Why not mix some sunlight and swimming with some kayaking or fishing?

1. Beach Brunnsviksbadet

Enjoy a popular beach and swimming area for families.

Ideal for: Couples, Families, and Budget

Brunnsviksbadet is a popular beach in Frescati Hage near Lake Brunnsvik in the Norra Djurgården area. The region has a tiny sandy beach, as well as various rocks and grassy areas with water access. On a hot summer day, the area can get very crowded, but for a bit more solitude, there are smaller swimming areas that are more sheltered in the surrounding area. People with limited mobility can make use of the guide rail that goes down into the sea. On the beach, guide dogs and assistance dogs are also welcome. To get to Brunnsviksbadet, take the metro to Universitetet and then walk 750 meters. The neighborhood is also easily accessible by bicycle.

- **Location**: Brunnsviksbadet, 114-19 Stockholm, Sweden

2. Beach Solviksbadet

Ideal for: Couples, Families, Budget, and Adventure

Solviksbadet is a huge beach with plenty of space for amusement, relaxation, and fitness. The area consists of a 150-meter-long sandy beach and some grassy sections. Children may enjoy swings and rockers, while adults can relax on park seats. The neighborhood also has Stockholm's first female-only nudist beach. Solviksbadet is an excellent alternative for anybody looking to stay active. The location is famous among divers since it is ideal for exploring beneath the surface and is a wonderful place to learn. There are also local workout paths and an outdoor gym. To get to Solviksbadet, take tram line 12 from Alvik to Smedslätten, then walk 800 meters down to the water's edge. If you want to come down by vehicle, there is parking nearby.

- **Address**: lstens Skogsväg 22, 16763 Bromma, Sweden

3. The Fredhälls Klippbad

Ideas for: Couples and those on a tight budget would appreciate this.

Fredhälls Klippbad is located on Kungsholmen in the Fredhäll area and is ideal for a swim. The area has a smaller grass and a wooden deck, as well as a café that serves coffee, lighter meals, and fresh buns throughout the summer months. The region is best suited for older children and adults because of the deep water and steeper cliffs. Because the region receives the evening sun, it's a fantastic place to end the day with a picnic and an evening plunge in the company of someone important. The location is easily accessible by foot or bicycle. Alternatively, taking the metro to Kristineberg, which is only a 10-minute walk from the water's edge, is the best option to arrive via public transportation.

- **Address**: Kungsholms Strandstig 602, Stockholm, Sweden 112 26
- Open from June to August, every day from 9 a.m. to 7 p.m.

4. Essingebadet, Lilla

Ideal for: Couples, Families, and Budget

Lilla Essingebadet is located on the northwestern side of Lilla Essingen, one of the city's smaller islands, and features an inviting jetty as well as a large grassy area. The location is appropriate for bathers of all ages and has a ladder that leads down from the jetty into the sea. For further safety, the swimming area is fenced off with a line and buoys during peak season. Lilla Essingebadet is set in lovely surroundings and is a nice place to catch some rays in the evening. The quickest way to get there is on foot or by bike. Keep in mind that parking in the neighborhood might be difficult.

- **Address**: Dagnyvägen 1, 11262 Stockholm, Sweden.

5. Beach of Flatenbadet

Swim in one of Stockholm's cleanest lakes.

Ideal for: Couples, Families, Budget, and Adventure

Flatenbadet is a picturesque region in the southeastern portion of Stockholm with a wide selection of activities for sports lovers of all ages. The beach is Stockholm's largest outdoor swimming and bathing area, and at about a mile long, there is plenty of room for everyone. Plunge into the ocean from the jetties or the diving tower, and stay active with the outdoor gym, beach volleyball pitch, boules court, minigolf course, and tennis courts. Explore natural habitats on the lake's walking pathways. Visit one of the outdoor terraces selling meals in the neighborhood if you want something wonderful to drink while relaxing in the sun or if your stomach starts to grumble after a workout session. Fladetbadet is easily accessible by vehicle and is located along Route 229. There is a spacious parking lot just at the front door.

- **Address**: Flaten, 128 30 Stockholm, Sweden

6. Blue Lagoon (Blå Lagunen) is a lake in Finland.

Ideal for: Couples, Families, and Budget

The Blue Lagoon (Blå Lagunen) is a picturesque artificial lake on the island of Munsön in Ekerö Municipality, with stunning turquoise waters that inspired the name. The lake was once a quarry, but it has since been filled with water and made into a popular swimming hole. A small ridge connects the pit to Lake Mälaren and a bigger dune to the north. Parking in the Blue Lagoon is occasionally prohibited due to unsustainable traffic congestion, so check the current rules before hopping into your rental car. When parking is prohibited, it is perfectly acceptable to walk or bike down to the lake and enjoy everything it has to offer.

- **Address**: 178 91 Munsö, Sweden, Blå Lagunen, Ekerö Kommun

7. Vinterviken

Look at intriguing structures, enjoy lunch on the grass, and then swim in the water.

Ideal for: Couples, Families, and Budget

Vinterviken has a park-like setting, ancient buildings, a lush garden oasis, and a little swimming cove. There's a little sandy beach and a wider grassy area where you may spread out your picnic blanket. Much of Vinerviken is made up of ancient manufacturing buildings that originally belonged to Alfred Nobel and are now listed and used for artistic and culinary purposes. The communal garden, Vintervikens Trädgård, is another lovely place in Vinterviken. Enjoy some peace in the lush surroundings, and why not stay for lunch? The most convenient method to get to Vinterviken is to take the metro to Aspudden, which is only a short walk from the water's edge. The neighborhood is also conveniently accessible by bike.

- **Location**: Stockholm, Sweden, Vinterviken, Hägersten-Liljeholmen

8. Långholmsbadet

In the heart of Stockholm, you may enjoy high-quality water.

Ideal for: Couples, Families, and Budget

Långholmsbadet is a centrally placed bathing location in Stockholm, having a 50-metre-long sandy beach and vast Grassy spaces shaded by trees and plants. The region has exceptional water quality and has even received a Blue Flag for the purity and safety of its waterways. Furthermore, the seafloor is sandy rather than stony. Långholmsbadet is located on the island of Lngholmen and is easily accessible from practically anywhere in town, with the neighborhoods of Södermalm and Kungsholmen about a half mile away. Because of the location, there are several cafés, ice cream stands, and restaurants for lunch. Långholmsbadet is easily accessible by bike, vehicle, public transportation, and foot.

- The address is Långholmsbadet 21, 117 33 Stockholm, Sweden.

9. Reimersholme

Find your own private space.

Ideal for: Couples and those on a tight budget would appreciate this.

The island of Reimersholme has several jetties and water ladders spread across the island rather than at a single designated bathing site. If the first beach you come across is in the shadow, it won't be long before you come across another that is in the sun. Out on the headland, there's a secret jetty and a grassy spot that's ideal for a solitary dip away from the masses. Because the swimming areas on this island are more spread out, it is ideally suited for adult bathers. Reimersholme is conveniently located in the heart of Stockholm, just south of Langholmen. Simply take the subway to Hornstull and then either walk or take the bus to Reimersholme.

- **Address**: 4 Pokalvägen, 117 40 Stockholm, Sweden

10. Hellasgården

Swim, walk and try your hand at other hobbies.

Ideal for: Couples, Families, Budget, and Adventure

Hellasgården is a popular and picturesque location in the Nacka Nature Reserve (Nackareservatet), with two lakes and a variety of activities. The big bathing facility at Källtorp Lake has broad jetties that provide an enclosed swimming area for children, as well as a BBQ area and large grassy fields. Söderby Lake, which is slightly smaller, features two sandy beaches, large grassy spaces, and rocks where you may relax after a swim. Hellasgården also provides opportunities to play football, and golf, hire a boat, and workout in an outdoor gym or on fitness paths. The location is only 15 minutes from Slussen's transportation center, making it simple to escape the hustle and bustle of the city and immerse yourself in beautiful and rich nature.

- **Address**: Ältavägen 101, 131 33 Nacka, Sweden

The 5 Best Subway Art in Stockholm

It is frequently stated that Stockholm's metro network is the world's longest art show, and the best way to see it is to stop at the 5 greatest metro stations in Stockholm for public art. The artworks frequently represent the local region that each station serves, and taking the metro is like traveling through Sweden's history from the 1950s to the present. Because the artworks were created over time, they vary greatly from station to station, but the overarching goal is always to make art accessible to the general people. More than 150 artists have contributed to the revitalization of around 90 of Stockholm's 100 metro stations.

1. T-Centralen

T-Centralen is a forerunner in metro art since it was the first station to be dolled up and continues to be a station with a diverse range of art. More than 21 different artists have been associated with the station since the first artwork was erected here in 1957. Materials and styles range from ornate columns and tiled/ceramic wall installations to vibrant paintings and cast-iron furniture. The blue line platform is wonderfully embellished with a blue ceiling painting by artist Per Olof Ultvedt, and one of the vaults depicts the workmen who initially built the station. T-Centralen is easy to get there because it is the central node where all of the city's metro lines intersect. The station is located in the Norrmalm neighborhood and is linked to Stockholm Central Station and the commuter station Stockholm City.

- **Address**: T-Centralen, 111-20 Stockholm, Sweden

2. Kungsträdgården

Check out this amazing rock-carved garden scenery.

The Kungsträdgrden metro station is frequently lauded as one of the most stunning of the city's stations, and it's easy to see why when you see its subterranean garden. Ulrik Samuelson, the station's artist, was inspired by the station's overground namesake, the King's Garden (or Kungsträdgården).

This is especially evident in the station's marble floors and several sculptures, while a petrified elm trunk in concrete recalls the elm species that stand above ground in the garden. For a true sense of being inside an archeological dig, head to the exit on Arsenalsgatan. The little peepholes in the wall will delight children, and adult visitors are encouraged to peer through them as well.

The Kungsträdgrden Metro Station is in the downtown Stockholm neighborhood of Norrmalm. From T-Centralen, take the blue line.

- **Address**: Kungsträdgården, 111 77 Stockholm, Sweden.

3. Rådhuset

Explore a bygone era via underground art.

Rådhuset is a famous 1970s metro station with full and fascinating settings rather than discrete artworks. It was vital to the artist Sigvard Olsson that the station's design and décor be reflective of what the surrounding region, Kungsholmen, was like in the past. A wall with baskets on it represents Kungholmen's history as a major market location, and one of the tunnels houses a variety of root vegetables. The hay on the walls depicts the farmers who used to come to Kungsholmen to sell feedstuff, while the petrified stack of wood harkens back to a time when the country was in crisis. The industrial period is represented by a massive chimney stack. Rådhuset Metro Station is located in downtown Stockholm on the island suburb of Kungsholmen. It is located on the blue line between T-Centralen and Fridhemsplan stations.

- **Address**: 25 Kungsholmsgatan, 112 27 Stockholm, Sweden

4. Stadshagen

The walls beside the platform of Stadshagen Metro Station are covered with corrugated metal artworks representing characters and events from Swedish sports. Lasse Lindqvist developed six distinct and intriguing wall installations. Walking through the many artworks gives the impression that the athletes are in motion, with different sceneries bursting to life depending on whatever direction you are heading in. For example, if you go in one direction, you will witness the Djurgården hockey team score against AIK, but if you turn around, it will be AIK who scores. In another portion of the station, you may see Ingemar Stenmark complete a race from start to finish. The first image displays a soccer match between Sweden and Denmark. Stadshagen Metro Station is located in Stockholm's inner city district of Stadshagen. The blue line serves the station.

- **Address**: Stadshagen 112 17 Stockholm, Sweden

5. Solna Centrum

Explore half a mile of political history in a commanding setting.

The Solna Centrum Metro Station is a tribute to themes that were very important in the 1970s. Karl-Olov Björk and Anders Åberg constructed a green spruce forest against a flaming red sky and filled it with scenes portraying 1970s subjects such as environmental pollution, deforestation, rural policy, and the latest craze to sweep the nation-running. Display cabinets illustrate events such as citizens gathered outside a business facing closure, a man watching as the natural nature around his cabin is damaged, and the Old Hagalund neighborhood with its exquisite wooden homes before they were regretfully dismantled. The blue line serves the metro station, which is near to the Solna Centrum Shopping Centre in Solna Municipality.

- **Address**: 171 45 Solna Centrum, Solna, Sweden

Stockholm's Most Instagrammable Locations

Sweden's capital is one of the most attractive in Northern Europe, with plenty of Instagrammable places ranging from majestic castles to edgy street art. The capital is rich in ancient districts and beautiful parks, but its most distinguishing characteristic is its abundance of water and hills. Quays, bays, canals, and lakes may be found in almost every neighborhood. This provides the city with a beautiful setting for pictures, with beautiful reflections sparkling in the lake after dark. Stockholm has its share of drab concrete, but the juxtaposition between the beautiful and the terrible is frequently intriguing, and the Swedish rain and fog will add a bit of intrigue and depth to your Instagram feed.

1. Stadshuset (City Hall)

Take a photo of the city's iconic silhouette.

Stockholm's majestic City Hall (Stadshuset), located on the island of Kungsholmen, and has become a symbol for both Sweden and its city, serving as the site of the world-famous Nobel Prize ceremony. In the Blue Hall, guests dine, while prize-winners and nobility mix and dance in the Golden Hall. Even the spire on this 100-meter-tall tower is golden, and the entire famous structure shimmers in the lake after dark. You may get a complete photo of the structure from numerous locations across the city, or take a short stroll from Central Station to get some close-up shots. An intriguing fact is that the City Hall was made to appear older than it is, harkening back to Sweden's history, namely the former Tre Kronor fortress.

- The address is Hantverkargatan 1, 111 52 Stockholm, Sweden.
- Open daily from 8:30 a.m. to 4:00 p.m.
- **Phone**: +46 8 508 290 00

2. Mäster Mikael's gata

Explore a beautiful neighborhood with a terrible history.

The scenic Mäster Mikaels gata and its historic surroundings are ideal for taking memorable shots both during the day and at night. The narrow street runs from Cornelis Park to Katarina Church and is close to Slussen Station and Medborgarplatsen Plaza. The historic public lift provides one of the most spectacular vistas in the city, standing in stark contrast to the modest wooden cottages and colorful paneled walls on Mäster Mikael's gata. Another contrast to the lovely atmosphere of the neighborhood is its history: Mäster Mikael was an executioner who was eventually executed himself. The notorious Catherine Fire also destroyed the area about 300 years ago.

- **Adress**: Mäster Mikaels gata 116, 116 20 Stockholm, Sweden
- Always available

3. In The Metro, There Is Public Art.

Admire the work that has gone into the metro's appearance.

The public art of Stockholm's metro system (or tunnelbana) is world-renowned, and it helps to brighten up what could otherwise be a pretty antiseptic setting. The many artworks, especially those buried underground, are all highly different from one another. The local transportation company describes its stations with enticing phrases like 'cave stations,' where jagged rocks are lightened up and painted in creative ways, or 'bathroom stations,' where tiles are utilized to create mosaics and wall art. Efforts to make the stations and subways more visually beautiful have been a feature of the network from its inception, with over 200 artists adding their touch. So get the SL Art Guide, go underground, and listen to fascinating stories about selected artworks at central stations.

- Phone: +46 8 600 10 00

4. The Gamla Stan

Captures stunning images in the capital's historic heart.

Gamla Stan is a photographer's heaven, and if all of its old buildings and charming alleyways weren't enough, the island's quay is a perfect site to capture the center. You won't be alone; the tourist destinations around the Royal Palace (Kungliga slottet), Stockholm Cathedral (Storkyrkan), and the street of Västerlnggatan are generally teeming with camera-toting visitors. Step to the side and you'll find small lanes, ornate building facades, and fascinating angles that make for interesting compositions. However, the fantasy neighborhood of Gamla stan has a terrible and bloody past. There are lots of locations to visit if you're interested in the city's macabre history - particularly on a gloomy day or a foggy evening. Keep in mind that photography is prohibited in many museums, businesses, and pubs.

- Always available

5. Riddarholmen

Discover a photogenic deserted and seldom visited island.

Riddarholmen is Stockholm's smallest neighborhood and is empty of people. The explanation is simple: its magnificent structures contain government institutions, courts, and offices. The Svea Court of Appeal (Svea hovrätt) and Riddarholmen Church (Riddarholmskyrkan), Stockholm's sole preserved medieval monastery, are among the most Instagrammable places. However, if you want to see the island's namesake, the House of Nobility (Riddarhuset), you must go to Gamla stan, which is the nearby island. Because of its central location, Riddarholmen is an easy site to visit on foot without having to fight through crowds. Riddarholmen, on the other hand, is a beautiful subject to picture from across the river, such as from City Hall quay (Stadshuskajen), where it appears as a postcard-esque silhouette reflected in the water.

- Always available

6. Bergian Garden (Bergianska trädgården) is a garden in Sweden.

The Bergian Garden (Bergianska trädgården) is a large, gorgeous, and plentiful botanic garden that is ideal for a series of colorful Instagram stories. It's conveniently accessible by rail or subway from Universities Station and next to the Swedish Royal Museum of Natural History (Naturhistoriska riksmuseet), so you may see both in one afternoon. A trip around this amazing landscape with walkways, bridges, and buildings by Brunnsviken Bay (Brunnsviken) does not require you to be very green-fingered. Don't miss the dome-shaped mansion Victoriahuset with its huge water lilies, the lovely ancient orangery where you can get a refreshing coffee, or the modern Edvard Anderson Conservatory with its stunning mini-landscapes with Mediterranean and tropical themes. Simply take out your phone when you see a man-eating plant, a coffee bush, or an enticing reflection in a glistening pond.

- The address is Gustafsborgsvägen 4, 114 18 Stockholm, Sweden.
- **Hours of operation**: Tuesday-Friday 11 a.m.-4 p.m., Saturday-Sunday 11 a.m.-5 p.m.
- **Phone**: +46 8 16 35 00

7. Graffiti Wall of Fame in Snösätra

A run-down industrial district has been converted into one of Europe's greatest legal street art displays thanks to contemporary graffiti on the street of Snösätragränd. Snösätragränd may seem like something out of a fairy tale, yet the area's isolation is one of the reasons graffiti artists began to flock here. The most convenient mode of transportation is thus by vehicle, while a ride on the metro will give you a greater taste of the amazing metropolitan experience that awaits you. Take the bus to Rgsved or Högdalen and walk for 15 minutes to Snösätragränd. When you enter, you'll see murals and paintings brimming with history and opinion.

Greta Thunberg and Pippi Longstocking stand cheek to shoulder with dinosaurs and war iconography in a one-of-a-kind setting where creativity reigns supreme. You'll even be able to pick up a paint can and make your addition.

- Address: Snösätragränd 1, 124 60 Högdalen, Sweden
- Always available

8. Drottningholm Palace (Drottningholms Slott) is a palace in Stockholm, Sweden.

Take a royal walk around a stunning world heritage site.

You won't be permitted to photograph the Swedish royal family at Drottningholm Palace (Drottningholms Slott), but the whole world heritage site is postcard-worthy. As you may be aware, the royal family does not dwell in Gamla stan, but rather on the more calm and beautiful island of Lovön, some 6 kilometers outside the city center. You may reach here via bus, bicycle, or a pleasant boat ride across Lake Mälaren from the City Hall wharf (Stadshuskajen).

Simply wander about the spacious park and baroque gardens, admiring the attractive structures like as the 17th-century palace, the Chinese Pavilion (Kina Slott), and the Drottningholm Palace Theatre (Drottningholms

Slottsteater). Keep an eye out for noteworthy events like the Christmas market and jubilee festivities.

- Always available:
- Phone: +46 8 402 62 80

9. Djurgården

Explore a well-liked tourism destination in the city.

Djurgården is home to several of Sweden's most popular attractions in one location, as well as a beautiful park-like setting where you may take photos. You may take the metro or the Djurgården Ferry, which is an adventure in and of itself, or simply walk over from the central area of Östermalm. The enormous Nordic Museum (Nordiska Museet) and the interesting Vasa Museum (Vasamuseet) are the first things you'll notice.

The Skansen open-air museum and zoo, the Gröna Lund amusement park, and many more thrilling places can be found deeper inside the island. If you want to get some fresh air, take a walk through the Royal National City Park (Nationalstadsparken) towards Waldemarsudde and Rosendals Trädgrd. And don't worry about getting hungry along the way; there are over 30 places to eat on this gorgeous urban island.

10. Katarina Lift (Katarinahissen).

View Slussen and Gamla stan from a renowned landmark.

The renowned Katarina Lift (Katarinahissen) with its breathtaking vistas greets visitors traveling from the city center to Slussen and Södermalm. The elevator not only relieves tired feet but also provides a magnificent night and day view of Gamla Stan and the city center. The beloved and functional lift building with its massive advertisements has seen several transformations throughout the years. It was recently refurbished and now features modern LED signs that show the time and temperature. If the lift is unavailable, walk the steps up to the famous observation platform, which is located above a posh restaurant.

- **Address**: Stadsgarden 6, 116 45 Stockholm, Sweden.
- Always available

EXERCISE

Which Of The Lake And Beach Are You Visiting, And What Are Your Experience Visiting The Beach Hope It Was Fun And Memorable?

_____
_____
_____
_____
_____
_____
_____

Which Of The Subway And Instargrammable Locations Do You Find More Attractive?

_____
_____
_____
_____
_____
_____
_____

CHAPTER TEN

Stockholm's Most Popular Neighborhoods

Sweden's capital has museums and cultural treasures, unrivaled big city atmosphere, and stunning natural beauty, but how can you know which of the cities many famous areas is ideal for you? There are commercial areas and gastronomic sections with high-end eateries. Not to mention the nightclubs, pubs, and arenas that hold major concerts, sporting events, and other spectacular events. If you want to escape the capital's frenetic urban pulse, there are lots of spots throughout the city where you may discover peace and solitude in green parks or along the water's edge. Discover and personalize Stockholm, the city of islands!

1. Norrmalm

Shopping and culture may be found in the center of Stockholm.

Norrmalm has an urban pulse, great shopping, and some of the country's most important cultural assets. In what is known as Stockholm's contemporary center, you'll discover boutiques and department stores to please even the most voracious of shoppers. Check out the flagship store of Swedish high-street mainstay hléns or at NK, both of which are situated in magnificent structures near Sergels Torg. The Kulturhuset Cultural Centre and the Royal Dramatic Theater (Kungliga Dramatiska Teatern) are both rich in culture. Norrmalm is located in the heart of Stockholm, just north of the ancient town, of Gamla Stan. It is home to Stockholm Central Station, hence there is no better district to be in.

2. Vasastaden

Vasastaden has a variety of parks that are ideal for a promenade as the sun sets, as well as several attractive eateries. This neighborhood is located to the north of Stockholm's most central sections and is home to the city's historic observatory, an extraordinarily beautiful and one-of-a-kind structure. Observatorielunden, a beautiful park with views of the city's rooftops, is just adjacent to the observatory. The large and majestic Stockholm Public Library (Stockholms Stadsbibliotek) is just a short stroll away from the park. Maybe you want something a little more contemporary and fast-paced? In that case, visit the Stockholm Museum of Video Games (Stockholms Spelmuseum), where you'll find all your favorite retro masterpieces in a tornado of fun and nostalgia.

3. Östermalm

An exquisite experience for the eyes as well as the taste buds

Östermalm is recognized for being one of Stockholm's most beautiful neighborhoods, with plenty of historical sites and delectable cuisines to discover and enjoy. Sample delicacies at the Östermalm Market Hall (Östermalm Saluhall), where you'll find anything from green smoothies to traditional fish meals, or visit the Swedish History Museum (Historiska Museet) to witness Viking weaponry and medieval paintings. Östermalm also has lots of shopping in the form of luxury shops surrounding fashionable Stureplan Square, and if you're looking for some verdant tranquility, head to the serene and quiet Humlegarden Park, which also houses the National Library of Sweden (Kungliga Biblioteket). Östermalm is located in the heart of Stockholm, a little over a half mile from Stockholm Central Station.

4. Norra Djurgården

Visit museums, see wildlife and learn about sports history.

Norra Djurgården is home to museums, open parks, and athletic facilities that are still in use today. The area is located to the north of Östermalm and is about a 10-minute metro ride from T-Centralen. After arriving, take a stroll around the lush Bergianska Botanic Garden to replenish your batteries. It's only a short walk from there to the large and majestic Swedish Museum of Natural History (Naturhistoriska Riksmuseet), which has a variety of intriguing displays ranging from extinct species to outer space. The Cosmonova, a combination planetarium and dome-shaped IMAX theater, is also housed inside the museum. The Stockholm Olympic Stadium (Stockholms Stadion) is located in the southern portion of the area. It was constructed for the 1912 Olympics and is the oldest Olympic stadium currently in operation.

5. Djurgården

Stroll around a lush island rich with wonders in the heart of the city.

Djurgården is a component of the Royal National City Park (Kungliga Nationalstadsparken), and the island is mostly made up of a lush park-like atmosphere, in addition to a variety of globally known landmarks. It's on the outskirts of the city center, less than 10 minutes by metro from T-Centralen Station - a fact that can be difficult to believe when surrounded by small-scale structures and an abundance of trees. Aside from greenery and wildlife, Djurgården is home to several of Stockholm's most well-known museums, including the Vasa Museum, ABBA The Museum, and Skansen, an open-air museum. If you and your trip companions are looking for a thrilling adventure, head to Gröna Lund, one of Sweden's most well-known amusement parks.

6. The Gamla Stan

In Stockholm's most picturesque area, you can feel the pulse of history.

Gamla Stan is Stockholm's oldest area, including some of the city's oldest and most magnificent buildings, as well as lots of places to buy and eat. This centrally positioned island in the city center is home to one of Europe's largest and finest preserved medieval centers. And strolling through its small and charming side alleyways will make you feel like you've gone back in time. Gamla Stan is lots of tiny shops, comfortable cafés, and good restaurants to explore in addition to the beautiful architecture. If you enjoy history, don't miss the Museum of Medieval Stockholm (Stockholms Medeltidsmuseum), the Royal Palace (Kungliga Slottet), the Royal Armoury (Livrustkammaren), the Nobel Museum, and other attractions.

7. Södermalm

Enjoy picturesque vistas and a laid-back attitude.

Södermalm is a pleasant and artistic zone where you can wander around and check out anything from quirky boutiques and comfortable cafés to the elegant Fotografiska (Museum of Photography). Södermalm is located south of the city center, about a 10-minute metro ride from Stockholm Central Station. Enjoy the breathtaking views from Fjällgatan on the so-called Heights of Söder, or attend an exhibition in the Göta Lejon Theatre. There are also several great restaurants in the area where you can end the day with a casual meal. Tanto Beach, located right in the heart of the city, is a terrific place to cool down in the summer.

8. Hammarbyhamnen, Södra

Witness a metamorphosis from old to new.

Södra Hammarbyhamnen is a perfect example of how to turn an old industrial zone into a fresh and modern district that oozes urban character. This region, located south of Södermalm and only 10 minutes by metro from Stockholm Central Station, is the place to go for vibrant performances and fantastic concerts at the famed Fryshuset venue. Come down in the spring to view the cherry trees in full bloom at Luma Park for a more serene experience. Surprisingly, Södra Hammarbyhamnen also has a ski slope where Stockholmers who crave the pure pistes of the Alps can experience world-class skiing without having to drive far.

9. Johanneshov

Attend an immersive concert or a tense match.

The city's arena sector, Johanneshov, is home to both the historic Globen Arena and the Tele2 Arena. The district is located south of Södermalm, on the opposite side of Årsta Bay and Lake Hammarby. Stockholm Central Station is about a 10-minute metro ride away. Johanneshov has witnessed world-renowned performers perform as well as massive, nail-biting games throughout the years. It is home to massive venues such as the gigantic, golf ball-shaped Globen Arena and its extension, as well as the Tele2 Arena, where musicians such as KISS and Elton John have performed and where several key Allsvenskan Football League clashes have taken place. Take a gondola over the roof of the Globen Arena for a somewhat different perspective on the sights afforded by this region.

10. Kungsholmen

Take a stroll along the water's edge and lunch at a quaint restaurant.

Kungsholmen is mostly a residential area, but it also has a plethora of intriguing restaurants, pubs, and cafés that are well worth a visit. The island is located west of the city center and is easily accessible by foot or subway. Kungsholmen is a terrific site for a walk along the water's edge since you'll get great views of the historic Stockholm

City Hall (Stockholms Stadshus), where the Nobel Banquet is dished out to all sorts of scientists and celebrities each year. Then, before finishing the evening in a bustling pub, stop by one of the neighborhood's quaint restaurants.

5 Essential Advice for Newcomers Visiting Stockholm Nightlife

Welcome to the city of Stockholm. During the day, it is trendy, energetic, and bursting with activity. There is an excellent combination of city living, nature, and waterfronts. Stockholm is not just a gorgeous city during the day; it also comes alive at night. So, if you want to get the most out of your nightlife experience in Stockholm, there are five essential aspects to master: location, transportation, pricing, guest lists, and after the club. This is for you if you're coming for the weekend and don't know where to begin. Five fundamentals for making the most of Stockholm's nightlife.

1. Location

Location, location, location is crucial! Södermalm and Stureplan are the two key neighborhoods to consider. The Södermalm neighborhood, located in the southern portion of central Stockholm and known as the "Brooklyn" of Stockholm, is ideal for a more casual feel with larger venue selections. Stureplan is home to huge clubs designed for enormous expenditure. They will have tougher door standards, commercial venues, and maybe lengthier lines. www.visitstockholm.com is a nice website to look for any pubs or clubs in Stockholm city. It is useful not only for recommendations but also for vital information for newcomers to the city.

2. Transport

On Friday and Saturday, trains operate continuously. This means that getting from the club to home is pretty simple, and transportation is typically available quite often. This also applies to night buses. If you live somewhere where you have to ride a commuter train, be sure you know what time the final trains are. All you'll need is a fully charged Access card, which you can get at any Metro station or convenience shop. It provides overnight access to both buses and trains. You will have two options: purchase credits, which work best for single voyages, or purchase a travel card (anything from 24 hours, 3 days, 7 days, and 30 days to yearly). If all else fails, you can always take a cab or Uber home.

3. Price

Right, let's get started. What is and isn't expensive is relative, so rather than telling you, I'll give you some context so you can gauge for yourself what to expect in terms of price. A cheap beer at a pub in Stockholm would be roughly 50 SEK, which equates to roughly 5 Euros, 4 Pounds, or 5 US Dollars.

Another option is to buy a few beers from your local Systembolaget and have a few with your friends at home before heading out, hopefully saving money on drinks throughout the evening and cutting down on bar expenditures. But honestly, how many times has that worked?

4. Guest lists

Guest lists are not just a quick way to skip the line; they are also a great way to get a discount and save money.

If you can, look for emails online and ask about group discounts. My favorite way to get on a guest list is a guest list app called Keyflow, which also has a website. Keyflow is becoming increasingly popular worldwide, with Sweden at the forefront of its success for a while now.

5. After The Club

If you're anything like me, this is the best part of the night: stuffing your face with hangover food after the club and stumbling into a kebab place. Around nighttime, Stockholm is full of options for kebab restaurants that serve both vegans and meat eaters. If all else fails, you can keep it simple with burgers at MAX or McDonald's, or a cheap hot dog at 7-Eleven.

To Summarize

Remember to plan, do your research, and have a general concept of how you want your night to unfold. The Golden Rule: proactive wins reactive, and having a little extra spare cash on hand for just-in-cases never hurts anybody.

Stockholm's Nightclubs

If you're looking for a full evening of pumping dance floors, hot DJs, mingling with nice people, and good drinks, you've come to the right place. For every age and taste, Stockholm has a ton of fantastic nightclubs. There's bound to be a venue that works for you and your group, whether you like to dance to the newest hit songs or house, pop, or soul music. Here is the guide to Stockholm's best clubs for a fun night out.

Discover The Best Nightclubs In Stockholm.

With its wide variety of bars and clubs, Stockholm offers something for everyone. From Södermalm to Östermalm, Old Town to Kungsholmen, and not least in the city center, there are plenty of places for everyone from hip club kids and pop nerds to those looking for a party at Stureplan or wanting to let loose to old favorites, and everything in between.

1. Stockholm Hyde

Hyde Stockholm is one of the most popular nightclubs in town, located in the exclusive mall MOOD. You can dance the night away in this exquisite venue, unwind with friends in cozy lounges, or just hang out at the bar where Hyde's talented bartenders are waiting to mix your favorite drink. The friendly staff delivers a high level of service and takes good care of you and your party. The highlight is the fantastic rooftop terrace (glazed in the colder s). It features four bars where you can socialize and drink while listening to amazing music from experienced DJs. In summary, if you're searching for a top-tier partying experience on a Friday or Saturday (other days closed), Hyde Stockholm is a safe pick.

- **Location**: Norrmalm/City, Jakobsbergsgatan 15,

2. Söder and Freyja

Great club atmosphere at high elevations where you may take in the city's charm from above. If that sounds appealing, you'll like Freyja + Söder, a significant investment by Stureplansgruppen.

The owners have worked hard to create an outstanding experience on Hornsgatan, and you'll sense it the moment you walk in. The finest party is held on the rooftop terrace of Söder, which has a capacity for 400 guests and has everything you could want - two excellent bars, a hot dog stand, and a breathtaking view over Djurgården, Old Town, Riddarfjärden, and Södermalm. Enjoy the sunset while reflecting on the nice things in life. Wine, beer, cider, non-alcoholic beverages, and excellent cocktails with quirky names that play on Södermalm and pop culture are all available. Who wouldn't like a Sommarkort, Bulleribng, or Blgeting?

Freyja, on the other hand, isn't all dancing, bar hopping, and entertaining events. There's also a great restaurant, which is the ideal way to start a night out. Take a seat in the contemporary and vibrant dining area, where they serve high-quality modern and straightforward food. When you and your guests have had your fill, proceed to the patio and continue the celebration.

- **Location**: Hornsgatan 18, Södermalm, Sweden

3. Hits in Golden

Golden Hit is a Stockholm nightclub classic and a favorite among people who wish to dance to tunes from the past and present. The disco balls are whirling, everyone is welcome, and the atmosphere is fantastic. The party has been going on since 1992, and at this entertainment establishment, you may not only have fun at the nightclub, but also see performances, eat and drink well at the restaurant with singing waiters (reserve a table in advance), and sing karaoke in the wonderful karaoke bar. In other words, it's all about entertainment.

Golden Hits caters to a little older crowd, and the facility features three wonderful dance floors with distinct themes. The schlager floor is on the main floor, where songs from Melodifestivalen and Eurovision are blended with Swedish pop classics. The nostalgia level on the middle floor has sing-along music and your favorite classics from the past. If you want modern house and urban music, come to the upper level's Biz club floor. There are five bars to pick from if you feel thirsty. In brief, Golden Hits is the place to go if you want a night out when anything may happen and the music you mimic in front of the mirror and sing to in the shower. It's unpretentious, a little sloppy, and a lot of fun.

- The address is Kungsgatan 29, Norrmalm/City.

4. Bron & Trädgården

Trädgrden, Stockholm's hottest outdoor club, is located beneath the Skanstullsbron bridge from the beginning of May until the beginning of September. A unique club experience has been developed in an abandoned location, attracting partygoers from all around the city. And news of the club's prowess has extended far beyond the borders of Sweden. Trädgrden is a place where you may dance to good music, interact with interesting people, drink beer from plastic cups, eat pizza, and watch live concerts by famous and lesser-known musicians. Alternatively, why not challenge your pals to a game of table tennis or boules? This is as near to a festival atmosphere as you'll find on a regular Saturday in Stockholm.

When the outdoor club is closed for the remainder of the year, you may attend the indoor venue Under Bron instead. The raw decor of this Södermalm nightclub, located in one of the buildings beneath Skanstullsbron, gives it an almost underground club ambiance that sticks out on the city's party scene. The dance floor is brought to life by well-known and yet-to-be-established DJs, and the room is filled with art in many forms. You may party till 5 a.m. because the club is open until then.

- **Location**: Södermalm, Hammarby Slussväg 2.

5. Fasching

Fasching is a favorite haunt of jazz, soul, blues, disco, and hip-hop fans. Since 1977, this popular performance venue, club, restaurant, and bar has been open. Since then, it has grown to become Scandinavia's largest jazz concert organizer (250-300 events each year), and the club is well-known both in Sweden and internationally. Almost every night, you may hear live music from major names to undiscovered artists, both Swedish and foreign.

On weekends, there are popular club nights in addition to concerts. Many iconic clubs have been housed at Fasching throughout the years, with the long-running Club Soul at the forefront. Since 1993, the club has provided Stockholm's most swinging dance floor with the greatest soul music from the 1960s and 1970s, and it is always filled. Club Afterglow runs the house on Fridays, and it's the natural pick for all R'n'B fans. The club plays a lively R&B blend of music from the 1980s to the present.

- **Address**: Kungsgatan 63, Norrmalm/City

6. Snaps

Snaps are a prominent Södermalm nightclub with a good position on Medborgarplatsen. The line is frequently long, and because of the extended hours, you may party here on both weekdays and weekends. The club is set in a wonderful historic edifice. The home was established in 1679, and much has transpired within its walls over the years, but it is now a restaurant, bar, and club. The venue boasts two party-filled floors, with the bottom floor resembling a castle cellar, complete with crystal chandeliers in the ceiling.

Snaps nightclub ups the ante throughout the warmer months. That's when the enormous, spectacular outside patio opens. It's ideal for drinking a good cocktail, catching up with friends, or simply getting some fresh air. Book a seat at the restaurant if you and your company wish to start the evening with a tasty supper that leads to a full evening at the club. The seasonal menu includes appetizers, burgers, pizza, and salads with southern European influences.

- **Address**: Götgatan 48, Södermalm

7. The Café Opera

Café Opera, sometimes known as "The Café," is one of Stockholm's oldest and most famous nightclubs, having been a part of the city's nightlife since 1980. It has a golden setting in the famous Royal Opera House, which was built in 1895, and beyond the red velvet ropes awaits a nightlife experience in one of the city's most gorgeous locations, with most of the original interior still intact. The venue, for example, has some outstanding ceiling murals.

You can always bet on a good time at Café Opera. There will be champagne, cocktails, occurrences, visitors coming in limos, and music to make you happy. Among many other things. Under the whirling disco balls, the audience is a terrific mix of Stockholmers and visitors who dance, party and interact. And if you're looking for a celebrity, chances are you'll notice one or two in the throng. Dress to impress in your best party attire and come to the Opera House.

- **Address**: Karl XII:s torg is located in Norrmalm/City.

8. Slakthuset

The Slakthuset neighborhood - Stockholm's "meatpacking district" - is located near the Globe, Tele2 Arena, and Gullmarsplan and is one of the city's most interesting locations right now. An old industrial area is being turned into an urban neighborhood, making it ideal for a nightclub with a raw industrial feel. Slakthuset, a former slaughterhouse, has been home to the club for numerous years.

Slakthuset has been a success since its inception, and its New York and Berlin ambiance draws partygoers from all across Stockholm. The nightclub has a capacity of 950 people and is separated into two huge rooms with numerous dance floors, allowing you to effortlessly change the setting and music whenever you like. The greatest electronic music is played by international DJs, who keep the dance floor moving. Aside from Slakthuset, this new cultural area also includes the performance venues Hus 7 and Slakthuskyrkan, the patio Kvarteret, and, last but not least, the 600 square meter roof terrace with wooden deck, which is a popular spot on beautiful summer nights. In other words, using the city metro is well worth it.

- **Address**: Slakthusgatan 6, Johanneshov, Sweden

9. The Amusing Duck

The Laughing Duck is located in the heart of Stockholm, just a short distance from the Central Station. It's renowned as the "never-sleeps" bar, and it certainly lives up to that moniker. Every day of the year, from noon until 3 a.m. (weekdays and weekends), it is crowded. The environment is calm, and everyone feels welcome - ideal for a great night out with friends or coworkers. Keep the spirit up with good DJs who have plenty of surprises in the record bins, and don't be shocked if there's a spontaneous dance in the bar.

The Laughing Duck is not just a nocturnal tavern, but also a restaurant and sports bar with eight large screens that display all major sporting events. Appetizers such as toast Skagen, buffalo wings, and nachos are available, as are hot dishes such as handmade meatballs, grilled salmon, fish'n'chips, spaghetti, burgers, and barbecues. If you are thirsty, the bar offers a wide variety of beers, cocktails, and other beverages. So, whether you want an after-work drink on your way home from work, a Saturday pre-party, or an entire evening out, you and your group will have a good time at The Laughing Duck.

- **Address**: Vasagatan 7 in Norrmalm/City.

10. Berns

Berns is located in the heart of the city, in Berzelii Park. It's a one-of-a-kind entertainment destination with a hotel, restaurant, bars, events, concerts, and one of Stockholm's greatest nightclubs in a well-preserved 18th-century Art Nouveau design. The expansive club space is essentially one enormous dance floor with unrivaled acoustics where you can dance the night away under massive crystal chandeliers. Make a night of it, beginning with an after-work drink at one of the bars and continuing the party on the contemporary dance floors.

Berns' nightclub is very renowned among music aficionados in the city. It frequently offers live concerts, and many well-known worldwide DJs visit to spin records. The London-inspired house club Le and the techno club Neu, which produces superb techno from the best sound system in the Nordic area, are two clubs that draw significant crowds. Also, don't miss Berns Terrassen, a terrace where you may enjoy stunning views while drinking a wonderful beverage.

- **Address**: Näckströmsgatan 8 in Norrmalm/City

11. Strand of Debaser

Debaser has been a part of Stockholm's nightlife since 2002 when he debuted at Slussen. They found a home in Hornstull in 2013, after several transfers, and their club and performance idea remains popular year after year. Almost every night, music fans and everyone else may enjoy performances by known musicians and up-and-coming stars in most genres, as well as talented DJs playing great music. Debaser also features the American pub Brooklyn, the Italian restaurant Capricci, and Pontonen, a beautiful outdoor patio on the river with a small live stage, in addition to the nightclub. In other words, everything you need for a complete Södermalm evening. Keep an eye on the website's program to ensure you don't miss anything. Tickets can also be purchased there.

- **Address**: Hornstulls strand 4, Södermalm

12. Kelly's Pub

Kelly Bar is a traditional rock bar that attracts partygoers of all ages. This pub-restaurant has a large following and a convenient position in Södermalm, near the busy Medborgarplatsen. Every day of the week, you can bring the group here and remain till 3 a.m. Begin the evening with an after-work or supper gathering, and then go all in until closing time. With reasonable food and drink pricing and a laid-back atmosphere, it's difficult not to have a good time.

The large venue provides lots of space for parties and is furnished in red with rustic wooden tables and cave-inspired décor that add to the rock bar atmosphere. Take a seat at one of the tables, relax at the bar, try your luck at the gaming tables, or dance anywhere you choose - Kelly's bar ensures a fun night out. They also open their outside patio in the summer, where you can relax with a nice beer and people-watch.

- **Address**: Folkungagatan 49, Södermalm, Sweden

13. The Mysterious Garden

The Secret Garden has been a famous nightclub in Old Town (Gamla stan) since 2014. This genuine and open-minded establishment, which has been rated one of Stockholm's greatest gay clubs, welcomes everyone. The rustic setting provides a bright, relaxing, and happy mood, and the courteous staff ensures that everyone feels at ease. The term The Secret Garden alludes to a secluded and intimate courtyard with a lovely Old Town vibe. Ideal for getting away from the hustle and bustle of city life.

The establishment is open from 11 a.m. until 3 a.m. and includes a restaurant and a bar. In other words, you and your group may begin and conclude the day here. Enjoy a nice supper in the courtyard or a glass of wine on the outside patio while watching the throng or the beauty of the sea before putting on your dance shoes and letting loose till the wee hours of the morning.

- **Address**: Kornhamnstorg 59, Old Town, Stockholm

14. The Soap Shop

The Soap Bar, located adjacent to Dramaten, is a prominent Östermalm nightclub that has drawn a diverse crowd of party-hungry Stockholmers and visitors since 1997. It's open till 3 a.m. Tuesday through Sunday and is a popular hangout for anyone seeking a joyful environment, tasty beverages, and dance-friendly music. In short, every night is a celebration.

There is also a lovely and well-stocked outdoor deck with an outdoor bar during the warmer months.

- **Location**: Östermalm, Nybrogatan 1.

15. Syntax Mistake Stockholm

Do you enjoy vintage games such as Street Fighter or Duck Hunt? Perhaps dancing to Commodore 64 8-bit music or ancient video games? Then you'll like Syntax Error, a monthly nightclub in Stockholm held at the H62 banquet hall on Mariatorget. It offers chip music parties where you may dance the night away to chip music (music inspired by the sound chips of the Commodore 64, Atari, Nintendo Entertainment System, and Game Boy, among other systems), beat your pals at old retro video games, or do anything you like.

Everyone is welcome at Syntax Error, the club for individuals who don't like the "common" clubs. The environment is welcoming and genuine - a true geek fiesta where you can be yourself. Dress yourself in your most recent cosplay outfit, construct impressive Jenga towers, or start a debate about your favorite Star Wars character. You will experience an amazing time.

- **Address**: Hornsgatan 62, Södermalm, Sweden

16. Spy Shop

Stureplan is undoubtedly Stockholm's trendiest nightlife zone, and the mysterious Spy Bar is one of the city's most famous nightclubs. The club, set in a historic structure in a prominent position, is undoubtedly one of the most famous in the Swedish capital, so anticipate lengthy lines and a hard-to-get guest list. But if you get in, you may party until 5 a.m.

Spy Bar features many stories, including the club on the second story, which seems like a vast turn-of-the-century residence. There are multiple bars in the rooms, as well as two dance floors where you may dance beneath the chandeliers. The nightclub's direction has shifted multiple times throughout the years. It now draws a diverse population, including those from the music and television industries. It's also a favorite haunt of Swedish celebs and influencers.

- **Address**: Birger Jarlsgatan 20 in Östermalm.

17. The Lemon Bar

Lemon Bar is a solid pick if you're searching for nightlife in Kungsholmen. This establishment has been open since 1994, and its extended hours allow you to party whether it's a workday or a weekend. You'll have a terrific time because the pleasant atmosphere has been their trademark since the beginning.

Lemon Bar is a fantastic find if you appreciate Melodifestivalen and Eurovision classics. One of Stockholm's top schlager bars, where it's nearly hard to remain still. Sing and dance to hit tunes till you can't anymore, then take a breather at a beautiful bar hangout with tasty beverages. You may start your night with a fantastic supper or after work because the bar shares its premises with Lokal Izakaya, one of the city's premier Asian fusion restaurants.

- **Address**: Scheelegatan 8, Kungsholmen

10 Cheap Ways to Visit Stockholm

Stockholm. It's one of my all-time favorite cities. I like its old architecture, the natural beauty of the archipelago, the crazy nightlife, and the kind of people that live there. Add in plenty of parks, beautiful cafés, and delicious cuisine, and you've got the recipe for one of the world's best places. I adore the city so much that I attempted to relocate there! I've made a terrific network of friends in Stockholm over the years, and I've been there so many times that I feel like I know it like a local.

If Stockholm didn't have polar winters (a tiny exaggeration), it would be the most ideal city on the planet. Because Stockholm (and Scandinavia in general) is pricey, many budget visitors avoid coming. There's no doubt that Stockholm is expensive in comparison to other European cities. However, a trip there does not have to break the bank. You may substantially reduce your spending and make the city much more inexpensive by following a few easy guidelines. That doesn't mean it'll be inexpensive, but these suggestions will help you stay within your budget as you visit this gorgeous Scandinavian city.

1. Participate in a Free Walking Tour

When I first arrive in a new city, one of the first things I do is go on a walking tour. It's the greatest way to learn about the city, visit the key attractions, and get answers to your questions from a local expert. Stockholm, like most other European towns, offers various free walking tours.

The greatest ones are offered by Free Tour Stockholm, which offers tours of the Old Town (Gamla Stan) that emphasizes the city's main views, history, and stunning architecture. English, Spanish, and German tours are provided. Each trip lasts around two hours and is free – just remember to tip your tour guide at the end!

2. Reduce Your Food Budget

While supermarket prices in Stockholm are comparable to those in other major cities throughout the world, eating out is quite pricey. As a result, I try to avoid eating out as often as possible. Fortunately, there are a few strategies to reduce your food budget without sacrificing quality. Cook your meals - Groceries in Stockholm may cost 600-700 SEK per week, which is a good deal considering the typical prepared dinner costs 125-250 SEK. Cooking your meals is far less expensive than eating out at restaurants. Willy's and Lidl are the cheapest grocery shop chains in town. Most Stockholm hostels provide kitchen/self-catering facilities (as do Airbnb units). If you intend to cook, find accommodations that will allow you to do so.

- **Avoid sit-down restaurants** - If you must eat out, stick to street food like pizza. Furthermore, Thai and Middle Eastern cuisine is typically relatively economical. Filling lunches may be found for less than 100 SEK. A simple lunch at a restaurant with table service would cost you closer to 200 SEK, so avoid them as much as possible. Also, avoid Drottninggatan (the city's major retail route) and sit-down eateries in Gamla Stan. Both are excessively expensive.

- **Try the lunch buffets** - If you're going out to eat, stick to lunch buffets. They typically cost approximately 120 SEK and are the most cost-effective way to eat out. Simply arrive early to avoid the crowds. Herman's and Hermitage are two of the greatest buffet restaurants in town. They both provide great home-cooked meals with a wide range of options.

- **Refill your water bottle** - Bottled water is pricey in Sweden, costing 22 SEK for each bottle! The city's tap water is safe to drink (and one of the cleanest in the world), so pack a reusable water bottle to save money. You can simply fill it up at most cafés. LifeStraw is my go-to bottle since it features a built-in filter that ensures your water is always pure and safe.

3. Take Advantage of Free Parking

Stockholm's parks are free, and there is free ice skating in the winter. You may also stroll through Gamla Stan and Södermalm and simply enjoy the city's splendor. They're a terrific location to unwind, picnic, read, and people-watch.

Djurgarden, Langholmen, Gärdet, and Ralambshovsparken are my favorite parks in Stockholm. They offer large open spaces and are ideal for a variety of outdoor activities or simply relaxing – especially on those long summer days!

4. Go to Free Museums

Museums in Stockholm aren't inexpensive, however, there are a few that are free (or have free hours). Here are the city's greatest free museums and attractions:

- Swedish National Museum
- Natural History Museum
- MoMA (Museum of Modern Art)
- The Swedish National Museum
- The National Maritime Museum
- The Medieval Stockholm Museum
- Swedish National Library
- The Museum of Ethnography

Check with the local tourist agency to see if any other museums provide free hours or exhibitions. They will have a list of all the free art exhibits and activities that come to town.

5. Reduce Your Alcohol Consumption.

In Sweden, alcohol is not inexpensive. Drink if you want to blow your finances. Reduce your alcohol consumption if you want your money to last a bit longer. Avoid wine (it's simply too expensive), avoid clubs (overpriced cover), and stick to lager, which is the cheapest drink available. If you must drink, limit yourself to happy hours. If you want to have a crazy night out, purchase your booze at

Systembolaget (the government-run liquor shop) and pre-drink to save money. Keep in mind that Systembolaget operates on a restricted schedule and is closed on Sundays.

6. Visit the Archipelago on a Budget

The Swedish archipelago is breathtaking, especially in the summer. Thousands of islands dot the landscape, and there are several excursions and trips available from the city during the day (or at nightfall). However, those excursions are not cheap.

Take the public ferries to the outer islands to explore and enjoy the archipelago on a budget. Tickets cost 50-150 SEK depending on which island you visit (day excursions cost 250 SEK or more). Use Waxholmsbolaget to find the cheapest tickets. If you're on a limited budget, try going during the shoulder season, which runs from October to March.

7. Purchase Transportation and Tourist Passes.

Stockholm metro tickets are expensive (38 SEK for each ticket), however, you can get an unlimited mobility card good for seven days for 415 SEK (plus 20 SEK for the card needed) (that's only 62 SEK per day). A 24-hour card costs 160 SEK, while a 72-hour pass costs 315 SEK. While the city is quite walkable, if you intend on riding the metro or bus, purchase a pass; all you need to do is utilize public transportation twice a day to give the pass a better deal than separate tickets. Get the Go City Stockholm Card if you intend on viewing a lot of sights or visiting a lot of museums. It offers free admission to over 60 of the city's most popular attractions, including sightseeing excursions, museums, and monuments. Single-day admissions cost 669 SEK, while five-day passes cost 1,569 SEK. While not inexpensive, you may easily save a lot of money if you do a lot of touring.

8. Make use of Hotel Points

Do you have any hotel points? Make use of them! When visiting an expensive place, travel hacking is the easiest method to save money, whether it's receiving free airfare or free lodging. Marriott, Starwood, and Hilton all offer properties in town that may be booked using points. Free is always preferable to paying.

9. Stay at a Low-Cost Hostel

Stay in the city's cheaper hostels, such as Lodge32 (there are cheaper hotels, but many have poor reviews; this is the cheapest hostel with a reasonable rating). This will save you up to 100 SEK every night, which will add up after a few days of seeing the city. You may also stay at City Backpackers, my favorite hostel in town. While not as inexpensive, they do provide free pasta (which can help you save money on meals) and a free sauna (which is simply a great amenity).

10. Make use of a Hospitality Network.

Because lodging in Stockholm is pricey, consider using Couch surfing. It's a website that links travelers with residents who give free lodging. Because there are many hosts here that participate in a highly active Couch-surfing community, you may save money on lodging while learning about the local culture. They host a lot of meet-ups (including weekly language exchanges), which is a terrific opportunity to meet new people. Even if you don't want to stay with a local, you may use the app to meet other visitors and locals for coffee, dinner, or a museum visit.

Airbnb is also popular in this area and is an inexpensive choice for those wishing for solitude but not wanting to pay for an expensive hotel. Visiting Stockholm does not have to break the bank. Sure, it's pricey, but there are several ways to save money here.

While it will never be dirt cheap, it may be economical if you plan and follow the recommendations above. Don't allow the pricing to deter you from visiting this undervalued and sometimes overlooked resort. It's well worth the money!

Book Your Trip to Stockholm: Logistical Hints and Tips

Book Your Flight

To locate a low-cost flight, use Skyscanner. They check websites and airlines all around the world, ensuring that no stone is left unturned.

Reserve Your Room

You may book your hostel through Hostelworld, which has the most inventories and the greatest pricing. If you wish to stay someplace other than a hostel, consider Booking.com since they constantly return the lowest rates for guesthouses and affordable hotels. My favorite locations to stay are:

- City Backpackers
- Skanstulls

If you're seeking more places to stay in Stockholm, here are some of my favorite hostels. If you're wondering where to stay in Stockholm, here's a neighborhood breakdown!

Don't Forget Travel Insurance

Travel insurance will cover you against illness, accident, theft, and cancellations. If something goes wrong, it offers complete protection. I never go on a trip without it because I've had to use it so many times in the past. My favorite companies that provide the finest service and value are:

- Safety Wing (for those under the age of 70)
- Insure My Trip (for those over 70)
- Medjet (for supplementary repatriation coverage)

Looking To Save Money with the Best Companies?

Check out my resource page for the greatest firms to utilize when traveling. I've included all of the ones I use to save money when driving. They will also save you money when you travel.

Best Shopping Locations in Stockholm

When you visit the 10 finest shopping sites in Stockholm, you'll discover anything from cheap garments to exquisite home goods. Sweden's capital has long been a shopping

Mecca in every sense of the word, frequently set against lovely surroundings such as the cobblestone alleyways of historic downtown Gamla stan. With each passing year, the Stockholm shopping experience has expanded to include everything from luxury shops to nostalgic stores. Not to mention all the massive out-of-town retail malls. Stockholm is a shopping mecca in practically every category, particularly fashion, design, interior design, handicrafts, and vintage items.

1. Scandinavian Shopping Mall

The Mall of Scandinavia is a vast retail center with 175 businesses, 43 cafes, and 15 cinema screens. This massive retail Mecca was erected in the out-of-town suburb of Arenastaden in the Solna satellite city to fit everything under one roof. It is accessible by commuter rail and tram, or you may arrive by automobile and park for free for the first few hours in one of the center's more than 3,700 parking spots. If you enjoy expensive goods and unique designs, don't miss the Designer Gallery. The Mall of Scandinavia is more than simply a shopping destination; it also hosts a variety of special events and has its app. Furthermore, the Mall of Scandinavia features a rooftop patio where you can eat or play table tennis.

- **Address**: Stjärntorget 2, 169 79 Solna, Sweden
- Open daily from 10 a.m. to 9 p.m.
- **Phone**: +46 8 4000 8000

2. Gallerian

Gallerian has a terrific position in central Stockholm, making it the ideal spot for a shopping binge while visiting the Swedish city. Gallerian has a fantastic location right in the middle of central Stockholm's primary retail district. The center even has its metro station, Kungsträdgrden. It is also easily accessible by foot. Gallerian is a great area to spend a couple of hours browsing the different stores selling anything from fashion to gadgets. Renovations and fresh arrivals attest to Gallerian's ongoing development. There is also a strong emphasis on pit stops, lunch, and supper, with a total of 25 cafés and eateries to select from. And how many retail malls have their health club, bouldering area, and rooftop patio on the 14th floor?

- **Address**: Hamngatan 37, 111 53 Stockholm, Sweden
- **Open**: Monday-Friday 7 a.m.-9 p.m., Saturday 9 a.m.-7 p.m., and Sunday 10 a.m.-7 p.m.
- **Phone**: +46 72 200 45 49

3. NK

NK is a world of fragrances, feelings, tastes, and information - a department store brimming with inspiration and individuality. The large and baroque-inspired edifice in the city center resembles a castle and is the ideal spot to have a drink of something sparkling while shopping. Throughout the store's illustrious history, exclusive debuts and celebrity appearances have been common occurrences. Browse unique brands or treat yourself to a touch of daily luxury. At NK, you'll discover the latest fashion for both men and women, as well as intriguing home decor, the latest trends, sports equipment, high-quality eating experiences, and much more.

- Hamngatan 18–20, 111 47 Stockholm, Sweden is the address.
- Its operating hours are 10 a.m. to 7 p.m. on Monday through Friday, 10 a.m. to 6 p.m. on Saturday, and 11 a.m. to 6 p.m. on Sunday.
- **Phone**: +46 8 762 80 00

4. Åhlén City

Åhlén City is the stunning flagship store of this well-known Swedish department store, with its own sweets counter and florist's section. Åhlén has locations throughout Stockholm, but when it comes to variety and location, their largest store is hard to top, located directly in the city center adjacent to all main transportation links. You may easily spend the entire day shopping at this award-winning retail center, discovering everything from fashion to interior design goods. And if you need a break, choose between a nutritious juice, a Neapolitan pastry, some decent health food, or some sushi. Alternatively, pick up some prepared meals and fresh ingredients from the store's well-stocked grocery area.

- **Address**: 50 Klarabergsgatan, Stockholm, Sweden 111 21
- Operating hours are 10 a.m. to 8 p.m., Monday through Friday, 10 a.m. to 7 p.m., and 11 a.m. on Sunday.
- **Phone**: +46 8 676 60 00

5. Sturegallerian

With its top brand names, famous eateries, fashionable nightlife, and public baths dating back to the 19th century,

Sturegallerian is a haven for genuine aficionados. It has a superb location on the busy Stureplan plaza in the fashionable area of Östermalm. The metro and buses stop just outside the retail center's doors, so getting there is simple. The stunning Sturegallerian is located in a beautiful structure with courtyards and basements, all done in a polished style with nothing left to chance. Stroll about in the company of award-winning and exclusive clothing, shoes, and accessories, as well as beauty goods and chocolates.

- **Address**: 114 35 Stockholm, Sweden, Stureplan 4.
- **Hours of operation**: Monday-Friday 10 a.m.-7 p.m., Saturday 10 a.m.-5 p.m., and Sunday noon-5 p.m.
- **Phone**: +46 8 611 46 06

6. Leading design boutiques on Birger Jarlsgatan

Birger Jarlsgatan is where all of the capital's most important flagship design boutiques are perfectly strung up like a string of pearls, gracing a street that separates the districts of Östermalm and Norrmalm. This opulent commercial district is known locally as the Library Quarter (Biblioteksstaden). The windows of design and home décor shops exhibit the proud products of talented Swedish artists and businesses, mostly aimed at the numerous visitors that visit each year. As a tourist to the nation, you will be surprised to see more rare and luxurious versions of the traditional goods you may already know and love from the cheap and cheerful IKEA. Discover all the current trends in Swedish and Scandinavian design by drawing inspiration from classic, nature-inspired, or innovative designs.

- **Location**: Birger Jarlsgatan, Stockholm, Sweden

7. Boutiques on Biblioteksgatan

Biblioteksgatan and the surrounding neighborhood have lately evolved as an elite retail district in Stockholm. Luxury retailers have opened their doors all along the streets of Biblioteksgatan, Birger Jarlsgatan, and Stureplan Square, and the neighborhood can now compete with many of the world's biggest metropolises. Previously, Swedish consumers had to fly to Copenhagen or London to fulfill their need for luxury and to wander among the world's finest fashion houses. Chanel, Prada, and its more easygoing Swedish rivals now compete in areas such as window displays and personal service. The region also has numerous more inexpensive stores that gladly coexist with the larger names.

- **Address**: Biblioteksgatan, Stockholm, Sweden

8. Vintage shops on Södermalm

Strolls are among the numerous unique and independent stores in Södermalm for a different shopping experience. The mountainous region of Södermalm is a large suburb that is located distant from all of the main hotels and the busier, more congested commercial districts. You may walk from Gamla Stan, take the train to Stockholm South Station, or use the metro. Bohemian Södermalm, or Söder as it's known to locals, has a calm and self-aware vibe and a wide choice of edgy boutiques with a focus on vintage, eco-fashion, charm, and personality. Don't miss the second-hand Mecca of Myrorna on Götgatan or the vinyl treasure trove of Pet Sounds on Sknegatan.

- **Location**: Södermalm, Stockholm, Sweden

9. Unique shops in Gamla Stan, Stockholm

Gamla stan, with its meandering cobblestone lanes and attractive shops, is a must-see on any visit to Stockholm. The capital's ancient, medieval heart pulses between the busy transit center of the City and the area of Södermalm, and is readily accessible either by bridge or subway. This picture-perfect 'city between the bridges,' as it is regarded by locals, is not large, but its many listed structures will pique the interest of inquiring tourists. Turn on your internal quality radar and set your eyes on authentic handicraft stores, vintage shops, and sure-fire winners like the bookseller Science Fiction Bokhandeln and the vinyl record store Sound Pollution. Diverge from the major sections of Västerlnggatan and Österlånggatan to locate hidden jewels and one-of-a-kind discoveries.

- **Location**: Gamla stan, Stockholm, Sweden

10. Stockholm Quality Outlet

Stockholm Quality Outlet is the place to go for a deal, with 30-70% reductions on brand-name products only a 20-minute drive from central Stockholm. Stockholm Quality Outlet is located near Barkarby Handelsplats, right off the E18 expressway, and provides free parking and a comfortable shopping experience. Get a decent bargain on over 50 prominent brands including Barbour, Acne, Hugo Boss, and Levis. The selection is extensive, with a strong emphasis on apparel, home, and cosmetics. If you prefer to visit design behemoths on their soil, Swedish home retailers like IKEA and Bauhaus are only around the corner.

- **Address**: Flyginfarten 4, 177 38 Järfälla, Stockholm, Sweden
- Operating hours are 10 a.m. to 7 p.m., Monday through Friday, and 10 a.m. to 6 p.m., Saturday and Sunday.
- **Phone**: +46 8 522 182 41

Shopping in Stockholm: 18 Amazing Swedish Souvenirs!

If you're considering a trip to Scandinavia, shopping in Stockholm for cool design goods and Swedish souvenirs might not be the first thing that springs to mind. That, however, would be a severe lapse on your behalf - and I'm here to ensure that you don't make it! Sweden's capital city is a great place to shop, whether you're seeking traditional Swedish goods and goofy ABBA memorabilia, or some modern Scandi design for your house. You may assume that there will be lots of stores in the city center, all having those wonderful objects you'll lovingly install in your home to recreate that homey Swedish style. Or you can do what I did and purchase a lot of slightly insane Swedish souvenirs featuring moose, tons of wonderful sweets, and a bunch of foodstuffs because that's how I roll! Let's face it: design goods are great, but everyone wants the fun stuff. Let's take a trip through the top retail districts in

Stockholm before we go shopping for amazing Stockholm gifts!

What are the greatest shopping places in Stockholm?

Stockholm shopping may be a big part of your trip, especially if you like the Scandinavian style. The city core, particularly the area surrounding the central station and Södermalm, with its stylish hotels and restaurants, is home to the flagship shops of several well-known Swedish brands. Department shops abound, with trendy products for your oh-so-chic flat that equal anything you can get in New York or Paris.

Although you don't want to spend your whole vacation walking around stores, even if they are amazing, it's well worth checking out some of the big shops when shopping in Stockholm. Design is a significant part of life in Scandinavia – l.ook at how IKEA took off over the world for one obvious example - and so viewing what local craftspeople have to offer is part of the Swedish experience.

Svenskt Tenn

Svenskt Tenn, located in Strandvägen 5, is most renowned for its lush textiles and wallpapers, but it began as a pewter manufacturer. Think Liberty of London, but with a cool Scandinavian touch. Understandably, you can find a plethora of wonderful pewter ornaments for your house, and if you have a substantial weight limit from your flight, they're great stuff to carry back - will anyone else get one? But the fabrics and wallpaper are where it's at: look wistfully at matching floral designs that are vibrant, brilliant, and not anything your grandmother would purchase.

Birger Jarlsgatan

Want to explore high-end shopping in Stockholm? Then Birger Jarlsgatan is the place to be! It's one of Stockholm's longest retail streets, and it begins immediately in the city center - if you're taking public transportation, use the Östermalmstorg metro station. This magnificent, tree-lined road with majestic buildings is home to some of Stockholm's top shops, including Gucci, Louis Vuitton, Prada, and every luxury brand you can think of.

You may even purchase a Rolls Royce from their northern end store! If you want to spend a lot of money, this is the place to go.

MOOD Stockholm

Looking for the greatest shopping center in town? Then you'll want MOOD Stockholm! This structure, located not far from the central station, is entirely dedicated to the pursuit of shopping pleasure. Stockholm inhabitants are notoriously stylish dressers, and here is by far the finest spot to pick up some Scandi fashion, with companies like Rodebjer and Maxjenny leading the way. Tired of shopping and trying on outfits? No problem: you may unwind in one of eleven cafés and restaurants before returning to the shopping.

Östermalms Saluhall

The Ostermalms Saluhall, a food hall that has stood proudly on this site since the 1880s, is a short distance from Birger Jarlsgatan. It's undoubtedly the greatest site in Stockholm for food shopping, and it's ideal for those on a tight budget. It's essentially a giant covered market where you can get some delicious fresh cuisine, including seafood from the icy northern seas! Traditional Swedish cuisine is the center, and you may help yourself to sample moose and reindeer meat. Try not to feel too bad around Christmas...

Gamla Stan

Although it is not a retail district, shopping in Stockholm would be incomplete without a visit to the city's Old Town. It's by far the greatest location for Swedish souvenirs (which we'll see in gorgeous, loving detail below!), but there are also a few nice sophisticated shops for the ardent shopper. Antique shops abound, as do beautiful craft stores like Makeri 14, fantastic toy stores like Krabat & Co, and economical outdoor gear at Slottshemmet. There are also several strange and interesting locations to explore - looking for a wig shop or a business specializing in stetson hats? You'll find them here.

What Are Some Nice Souvenirs To Bring Home From Stockholm, Sweden?

Now, on to the big event! As much fun as shopping in Stockholm for contemporary textiles and homewares is, exploring the shops for the oddest Swedish souvenirs is where it's at! Except for a handful of entries, all of the items listed below are available in the stores of Gamla Stan, Stockholm's Old Town, so you won't have to travel far. You'll surely be visiting here and strolling through its charming streets, so stock up on Stockholm souvenirs and

Swedish presents while you're there! How's that for efficiency?

1. Viking Trinkets

What shouts "Swedish souvenirs" to you? Something that reminds you of the country's pleasant people, who chirp "hej hej!"When they meet you? No, we glorify their violent, plundering past! Vikings have always been popular (which says something about mankind), but with current television programs bringing them back into popularity, you'll find Viking-themed presents all over the city. Viking keychains, Viking candle holders, and cute cuddly toy Vikings. But if you want something that truly evokes the spirit of yesteryear, go no further than Handfaste. This cool small boutique offers everything your pillaging heart could desire, from Viking-inspired jewelry to horn combs and troll crosses, which you can use to keep trolls away from your house. Useful! Their products are quite well-made, and the jewelry is truly stunning. There are also a surprising number of products that are helpful, such as housewares and even scissors and nails. It's also fun to gaze at the replica weapons and armor, even if your budget won't allow you to purchase them. Shopping in Stockholm has never been so much fun!

2. Mustard

Food shopping in Stockholm is simple and pleasurable (I can't think of any country with such fantastic supermarkets), and it's a surprisingly nice way to pick up some yummy Swedish souvenirs. But there is one item you must not forget to include on your shopping list. Mustard is one of the greatest Swedish gifts available. No way. A tube of Slotts Senap is a must-have for a country obsessed with the ideal hot dog. Believe me, the mustard lovers in your life will fall on their knees and thank you for exposing them to this stuff.

Slotts is the traditional Swedish mustard, albeit there are a few rivals. It's spicy without being overpowering, and if you want to reproduce the hot dogs you had during your visit - whether they were the irresistible ones from Pressbyrån or classier cuisine from eateries like The Hairy Pig - this is the thing to acquire. It's also simple to obtain when shopping in Stockholm, as there's no need to travel to some outlying grocery.

Simply go to the Coop at the southern end of Gamla Stan to find a variety. Put it on your hot dogs, take a bite, and you'll be transported.

3. Swedish Meatballs

I have an undying love for Swedish meatballs. I've even published a guide on where to locate the greatest meatballs in Stockholm. Although you may not have considered bringing meatballs back home, there is no reason why you can't include them on your list of Swedish mementos, as long as you don't go overboard! They're pre-cooked, so you shouldn't have any trouble packing a pack or two, and they make fantastic Swedish presents for anyone who's never been to Sweden! And I won't criticize you if you keep them for yourself, because I did.

They're often prepared with ground pig and beef and are also quite easy to get when shopping in Stockholm. The Coop in Gamla Stan offers a decent range, and you can even get a gravy mix to go with them. The directions are (understandably) in Swedish, but I ran them through Google Translate and found them simple enough to follow! Want more incentive to bring this home as Swedish souvenirs? They're safer to travel than certain local delicacies - picture-packing pickled herring in your bag. Consider this for a moment. Swedish meatballs all the way? Yeah, me too.

4. Christmas Decorations

Going shopping in Stockholm in the winter? Then Christmas decorations are the ideal Swedish keepsake!

You may buy these tiny beauties for yourself, but they also make a great present. Consider the joy of receiving a tree decoration from afar and being able to place it directly on your tree. Isn't it pretty? They're ideal stocking stuffers, especially when your charming little ornament is a murderous Viking! Yes, although there are a wide range of decorations available in almost every shop in Gamla Stan, Viking decorations have to be the pinnacle of Swedish Christmas presents. Handfaste, a trusted Viking paraphernalia shop, provides the greatest assortment, including traditional winter symbols as well as beautiful small wooden cut-outs. Otherwise, visit some of the artisan businesses along Västerlnggatan, such as Made in Stockholm, which has an incredible selection of locally-made items (with delightfully joyful staff!). Shopping in Stockholm is enjoyable at any time of year, but walking around Christmas markets and purchasing handcrafted Swedish goods has to be the pinnacle. And your top priority list item should be Christmas décor.

5. Knäckebröd

"What the eff is knäckebröd?"", you may be wondering. To answer your query, it's crisp bread - but you'll recognize it most as that tasty food you've been served alongside your meals if you've been eating out in Stockholm! The Swedes have been making crisp bread since 500 AD, and as a result, they're excellent at it. Rather than serving your meals with plain old standard bread, crisp bread is brought nice and fresh, and it's a fantastic compliment! I ate a lot of Swedish meatballs in Stockholm, and the basic, cracker-like texture provides a nice counterpoint to all those explosive flavors. You'll want to bring some home with you, and while they're not the type of Swedish mementos you'll present to your family, they're perfect for adding a simple remembrance of your holiday to your evening meal.

The Coop in Gamla Stan is once again the greatest location to get knäckebröd (and one of the nicest places to shop in Stockholm!), and you'll have to make a decision. You may buy a big wheel of knäckebröd - approximately the size of a platter but surprisingly light - or smaller, wedge-shaped packages. I like the smaller wedges because crisp bread tends to get stale shortly after opening the packet, so unless you have an airtight container to store it in, you'd be better off investing in a pair of wedges.

Tip: Place it in a plastic bag before putting it in your baggage; otherwise, you'll be hoovering crisp bread crumbs out of your clothing for weeks. Take it from personal experience.

6. Lingonberry jam

Is there anything that sums up a trip to Sweden more than lingonberry jam? It's not quite the same as the fresh, tart lingonberries you'll have eaten with your Swedish meatballs, but it's the next best thing! It should be illegal to go shopping in Stockholm without bringing back a jar of this (don't worry about breakages - cover it in a plastic bag and a towel and it'll be OK). The lovely inhabitants of the city even regard this as one of the greatest Swedish souvenirs available: you'll find it in numerous shops. After all, if you're bringing back Swedish meatballs, why not bring back the jam to go with them? The taste combination is one of the greatest I've had - the rich, gravy-laden meatballs contrast so dramatically with the lingonberries, yet it works!

Although every Swedish shop worth its salt should sell lingonberry jam (the reliable Coop in Gamla Stan does), I purchased mine from Skansen's gift shop. This fantastic ethnographic park has a fantastic store just outside the gates, so you don't even need to enter the park to obtain access to it. It sells a broad variety of Swedish crafts, such as hand-carved wooden items, woven blankets, and household products. More significantly for us, it sells great lingonberry jam, and the kind staff will wrap it in cardboard for extra protection! By the way, visit Skansen itself, not just the shop - it's fantastic!

7. Winter Woolens

If you're visiting Stockholm in the winter and forget to bring enough warm gear, you're in trouble. So acquire some warm Swedish woolies as one of your first stops when shopping in Stockholm! They also make fantastic Swedish souvenirs, so everyone wins! Look for some mitts in particular. Sweden adores its crafts, and Lovikka mittens are at the top of the list. These hand-warmers are made in a tiny hamlet in northern Sweden and are particularly built to resist the extreme cold of winter in northern Sweden (if you think Stockholm is cold, you haven't seen anything yet). They follow a very tight design that was designed by a woman from a poor background who was a total knitting legend, and they frequently contain some traditional designs. What more could you want in a Swedish gift?

Genuine Lovikka mittens may be found at Svensk Hemslöjd, a shop so fantastic that you'll want to toss your credit card at them right away. And you might need to because true Swedish crafts aren't cheap. You can expect to pay around 895,000 SEK for a pair (around USD 90), so be sure you want one. If you're cheap like me, you can remain warm Scandi style! Many of the souvenir stores in Gamla Stand sell bundles of woolens that include a hat, scarf, and mittens - they're touristy, but they're still decent quality! I got a pack with a woven moose on it, and they've kept me warm all winter. They're thermal-lined and a great alternative for shopping outside in Stockholm!

8. Swedish Candy

What is the principal purpose of a newsagent? To stay up with the news? To offer necessities like stamps and the like? Forget that: for those looking for Swedish gifts, these locations are ideal areas for delectable Swedish confectionery! Swedish confectionery is well-known for its quality. When my dear friend Ina gave me a care package of famous Swedish items, sweets, and candies grabbed center stage, and I enthusiastically devoured the bunch. And newsagents like Pressbyrån and 7-Eleven are the ideal places to get them; they often offer a better range than supermarkets. You may also buy other tasty Swedish delicacies like ginger cookies and Ramlösa fizzy beverages!

So, which sweet should you get? Everyone is aware of Daim bars, which are undoubtedly the most well-known of Sweden's chocolatey offerings, but don't overlook Marabou. This chocolate company has a vast variety, including chocolate paired with the Swedish national love of licorice, and it's always wonderfully smooth. My personal favorites are the little rolls of mint-flavored chocolate buttons, which are ideal for storing in a backpack and munching on throughout the day! Dumle toffees come in a bag and are similarly Moorish. Are you more into fruit gums? In such a case, you should certainly look at Bilar's product line! The regular edition of these car-shaped sweets is pillory marshmallows that melt in the tongue. My favorites are the Fruktcombi ones!

9. Polkagris

When shopping in Stockholm, make a trip to Gamla Stans Polkagriskokeri on Stora Nygatan. This isn't only a chance to buy Swedish trinkets. This is where you'll find the freshest, most delicious candy you've ever eaten. Polkagris is a delicious delicacy that is akin to British coastal rock. It's hard, peppermint-flavored candy, yet the flavor is subtle, leaving you wanting more and more! It's also a fairly strange name, given that it translates as "polka pig"; there's also some conjecture that it's related to Poland, given that it's generally red and white. But who cares? All that matters is that it's wonderful, sugary, and will keep your favorite sugar lover calm for hours.

Gamla Stans Polkagriskokeri is the home of polkagris in Stockholm - go in and you'll be hit by the aroma of cooked sweets. Yes, it is manufactured right in front of your eyes! Standing near the kitchen, you can see huge ropes of sugar being laid out and flavored and colored before being chopped into manageable bits. Want to try before you buy? Not an issue; the staff frequently brings over freshly prepared samples. I had polkagris, which was still warm and squidgy. I tried some extremely fresh fudge. You can bet I purchased a pack of both since they were so delicious. This is essentially the candy store of your dreams.

10. A Dala Horse

If you go shopping in Stockholm, you'll notice small red Dala horses in any of the businesses selling Swedish gifts. If you can locate one that doesn't sell them, I'll give you a big imaginary prize, since these tiny fellows are everywhere! Purchasing a carved wooden dala horse is a rite of passage for every tourist to Stockholm, and I have no issues because they're freaking lovely. They originated in Dalarna, a region north of Stockholm that borders Norway, and were initially little wooden toys for children to play with. Because Amazon deliveries were few in 1716, dedicated Swedish fathers fashioned the toys out of scrap wood and a whittling knife. I don't know about you, but that makes me want to burst.

They affected all those youngsters, for the Dala horse quickly became Sweden's national toy. Although they are available in a range of colors at Stockholm souvenir stores, they are normally red with a blue, white, and green traditional design painted on to resemble a saddle and bridle. It's sort of fascinating to think that they were initially manufactured from scrap wood from furniture production and that they're now among the most iconic Stockholm souvenirs! You'll have little trouble discovering Dala horses in any of their guises. Walking down Västerlnggatan, you'll see not only the carved wooden horses, but also Dala horse keychains, t-shirts, and cuddly toys. I bought one of each!

11. Moose-related Presents

When looking for Swedish gifts in Stockholm, one species stands out above the others. Yes, even more than Vikings! And that beast is the common moose. If you walk into any shop in the city center, you will be attacked with moose on every form of souvenir conceivable. Socks? Check. Cuddly toys? Check. Magnets for the refrigerator? Check. Thermal blankets? Check. But I'm not going to complain since there's something very endearing about moose, and seeing their somewhat dopey expression on any number of Swedish presents never fails to delight me. They're also a wonderful poster child for Swedish nature, which offers many more intriguing creatures than you probably imagined!

Yes, when you visit Sweden, you won't simply be sharing the nation with a lot of moose - or elk, as they're more frequently known in Europe. Brown bears, wolves, lynx, wolverines, and some exceptionally nasty squirrels (well, I lied about the last one; they're as sweet as buttons) may be found in the country's harsher areas. So acquiring a few trinkets depicting Sweden's rich fauna is a wonderful reminder that this extremely contemporary nation nevertheless manages to strike a balance and protect its natural heritage. I'm not sure about you, but I think that's worth celebrating. In Stockholm, get up some moose-related gifts and remember their wild cousins!

12. Cloudberry Jam

Cloudberry jam is one of the finest Swedish souvenirs you've never heard of! Cloudberries aren't well-known outside of their northern homelands because they're predominantly wild berries. They're famously difficult to produce, so they're usually left to do their thing in the wild before being plucked by enthusiastic Scandinavian berry hunters and converted into jam and alcoholic drinks.

They typically taste sour, like a mix between a raspberry and a red currant. They're also considered a super food because they're loaded with vitamin C! Swedes enjoy putting cloudberry jam on ice cream because the acidity and fruitiness contrast wonderfully with the smooth vanilla - you'll almost certainly try it at one of Stockholm's restaurants! If you'd rather take a jar home to splash over your favorite gelato, visit the gift store in Stockholm's City Hall. It's not the largest gift shop in the world, and it may get a little crowded because it's also the waiting room for City Hall tours (which you should take), but it offers some fantastic items! It's a must-see when shopping in Stockholm!

13. Sami Bracelets with Designs

Still in Stockholm City Hall? Looking for some classic Swedish gifts for the fashionista in your life? Something handmade that represents the country's culture? You're in luck! While you're getting your cloudberry jam, check out the selection of patterned Sami bracelets, which are often crafted from reindeer leather and pewter wire. The patterns may appear faintly familiar: the old ones, particularly the overlapping loops, are so distinctive that they've been replicated repeatedly in current designs. These bracelets, on the other hand, are authentic!

The native inhabitants of northern Norway, Sweden, and Finland are known as Sami. They are descended from Sápmi (also known as Lapland). There is still a history of making a livelihood from reindeer herding, and as a result, Sami crafts most typically employ reindeer leather as a base for their crafts. When shopping at Stockholm stores, you may get handcrafted leather purses, boots, and belts (expect to pay a premium for everything handmade), but bracelets are by far the most popular item. They're a little less expensive, and they're a great way to remember your time in Sweden! If the price of a real Sami bracelet is still a little steep, the City Hall now sells patterned bracelets without the detailed Sami metal design. They're made of woven cloth mounted on reindeer leather and are a considerably more economical option!

14. Wooden Butter Knife

Has all this shopping in Stockholm made you want to redecorate your home in that cool Scandi design style? That is perfectly understandable. But there is one item you will need in your kitchen to finish it: a wooden butter knife. These are the most common and inexplicable of Swedish souvenirs, and you'll find them EVERYWHERE. I mean, a lot of Stockholm souvenirs and Swedish presents are understandable. Everyone understands t-shirts, key chains, and food things. But why are wooden butter knives so popular in souvenir shops?

The Swedes like butter and have expended tremendous effort in developing the best butter knife imaginable. After all, how can you properly appreciate butter unless you have a good butter knife? Knives made of metal or plastic just do not cut it - the butter knife must be natural, supple, enable the greatest amount of smooth spread age, and ideally be fashioned from trees in the depths of old Swedish woods. Then, and only then, will you have paid respect to the magnificence of butter. Why are butter knives so popular as gifts in Stockholm? Because the Swedes have perfected the art of butter spreading and want you filthy heathens to taste it for yourself. It's fairly nice. Visit Skansen's gift shop to get a high-quality wooden butter knife!

15. ABBA Presents

If you travel to Sweden, you will become an ABBA fan. It's unavoidable. When you go shopping in Stockholm, you will quickly become infected. You might not have paid much attention to ABBA before - you might be one of those individuals who think "Yeah, Dancing Queen is alright" - but you'll leave rabidly obsessed. It might be as easy as stepping into a shop to get some Swedish goods and hearing them on the radio. You immediately realize, "Wow, they were good." They're so sweet, talented, and Swedish." BANG. They've got you. The next thing you know, you're seeing ABBA documentaries on television. It happened to me.

If you're an ABBA fan, what else can you do than visit Stockholm's ABBA Museum and load up on tacky souvenirs that you'll love and despise at the same time? I Heart ABBA t-shirts, ABBA Dala horses, ABBA lip balms, and a wonderful picture of Bjorn are all here, brilliant and vibrant, ready for you to take them. Oh, ABBA, how can I resist you?

16. Socks

Socks may not be the first item that comes to mind when thinking about things to buy in Stockholm. But it's true: every Swedish souvenir shop will have shelves and racks of socks. I'm not sure why, and I can't locate any tales on the Swedish obsession with socks, but there you have it. It's not only Stockholm; I went to Gothenburg and discovered the same thing. Socks everywhere! Still, who's complaining? Socks are a useful keepsake (particularly if you failed to bring enough with you) and a pleasant, uncomplicated Swedish present to carry home for someone else. You can even store them for Christmas to change things up! There are lots of colorful socks with moose motifs - because many Stockholm souvenirs have moose motifs - but also some very lovely ones with the Swedish flag. If you don't want to flaunt your love of a location by wearing a t-shirt, you may hide it in your socks. Plus, who needs a reason to purchase wacky socks? No, we say!

17. Kosta Boda Glass

If you're looking for a classy Swedish memento, look for a Kosta Boda glass when you're shopping in Stockholm! Take a peek at their website to learn what makes this kind of glass so unique. Click on Stemware and ready to be astounded at what you can accomplish with a piece of glass! Their glasses have the most vibrant, interesting patterns, and they're perfectly ideal for any home - there's truly something for everyone. My particular favorite is the

Mirage vases, which appear nearly petrol-colored. I adore them! I'm usually a fan of taking back wonderful, well-crafted glass and crystal as mementos from Prague and Budapest, but the work at Kosta Boda could be some of the most eye-catching I've seen! Kosta Boda may be found at a variety of Stockholm stores, including Cervera and Wasa Crystal. If you like department shopping, consider Nordiska Kompaniet, which is located near the central station!

18. Licorice with

a Salty Aftertaste

Did you know that licorice originated in warm regions such as India, Iran, and even Italy, although it is most popular in the colder areas of northern Europe? It's true! If you go shopping for Swedish souvenirs in Stockholm, I bet you'll discover a metric ton of salty licorice. There are entire licorice emporiums devoted to it, and as I discovered, they're still bustling at around 6 p.m. I foolishly purchased a package of fruit gums from a newsagent and was astonished to discover that the black sweets were licorice, not blackcurrant! (Which surprised me considering I don't like the stuff?)

If, like me, you have a licorice fanatic in your life, you should go to a branch of Lakritsroten, which describes itself as licorice heaven - and they surely offer every variation you can think of! You're guaranteed to find your favorite gummy here, whether it's hard, soft, sweet, or salty. If you want to be sure you obtain Swedish presents for your loved one, they conveniently organize everything by nation of origin. So, if you want some licorice from nearby Finland or Italy, you may! It may not be everyone's cup of tea, but it is undeniably Swedish!

DID YOU SMILE TODAY?

EXERCISE

Do You Plan To Visit Any Of The Neighborhoods, If Yes Which Are You Planning On Visiting?

_____
_____
_____
_____
_____
_____

Are You Visiting For The First Time, If Yes Hope The Guide And Advice Are Helpful?

_____
_____
_____
_____
_____
_____
_____
_____
_____

The Nightclubs Are Worth Visiting If You Visited Any Of The Above Mention What Are Your Experience And Thought?

_____
_____
_____
_____
_____
_____
_____
_____
_____

Hope The Your Planning Process And Budget Are Well Plan With The Cheap Ways To Visit Stockholm And The Logistical Hints And Tips Hope They Were Helpful In Booking Your Trip?

_____
_____
_____
_____
_____
_____

Don't go back home without getting souvenirs for friend family and love ones. What are you thinking of buying as a gift?

BECKY'S GUIDE

If you enjoy this guide and it was helpful to you or you've any questions, kindly send a message via email

beckyrhodesguide@gmail.com

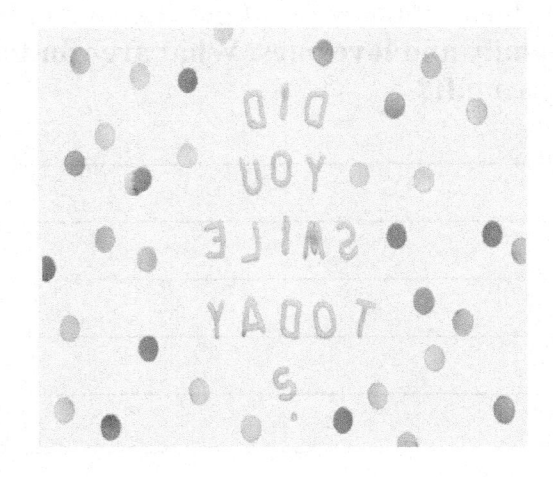

Made in the USA
Las Vegas, NV
21 April 2025